The CRAZIEST BOOK OF JOKES

with Glen Singleton

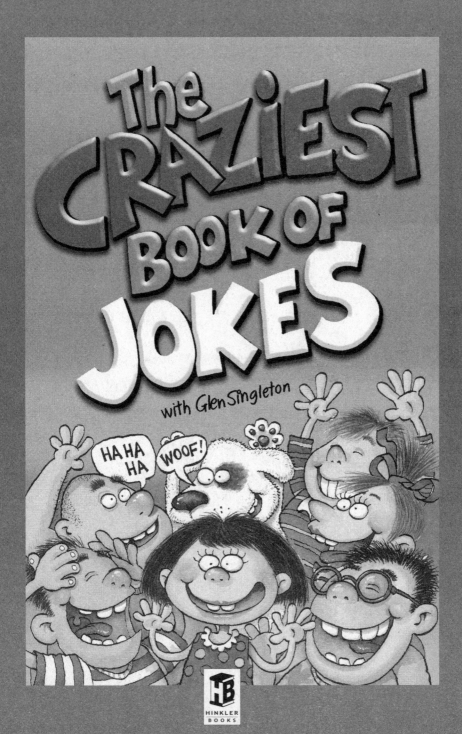

HA HA HA   WOOF!

HB
HINKLER
BOOKS

Cover Illustrations & Illustrations: Glen Singleton
Typesetting: Midland Typesetters, Maryborough, Victoria, Australia

 The Craziest Book of Jokes
Published in 2004 by Hinkler Books Pty Ltd
17-23 Redwood Drive
Dingley VIC 3172 Australia
www.hinklerbooks.com

ISBN 1 7412 1506 4

Printed and bound in Australia

contents

Jokes and Riddles

What are two things you
cannot have for breakfast?

Lunch and dinner.

What has eyes that cannot see, a tongue that
cannot taste, and a soul that cannot die?

A shoe.

What can you hear but not see and
only speaks when it is spoken to?

An echo.

How many apples can you put in an empty box?

One. After that it's not empty anymore.

When will water stop flowing downhill?

When it reaches the bottom.

What's easier to give than receive?

Criticism.

What's red and goes up and down?

A tomato in an elevator.

Why do firemen wear red braces?

To keep their trousers up.

When do clocks die?

When their time's up.

What kind of dress can never be worn?

Your address.

What word is always spelt incorrectly?

Incorrectly.

What has a bottom at the top?

A leg.

What's an ig?

An Eskimo's house without a toilet.

What's the last thing you take off before bed?

Your feet off the floor.

What is always coming but never arrives?

Tomorrow.

What can you serve but never eat?

A volleyball.

What do you put in a barrel to make it lighter?

A hole.

What stays in the corner and travels all around the world?

A postage stamp.

Who was the fastest runner in the whole world?

Adam, because he was the first in the human race.

How does a fireplace feel?

Grate!

What gets wet the more you dry?

A towel.

What's green, has eight legs and would kill you if it fell on you from out of a tree?

A billiard table.

What breaks when you say it?

Silence.

What bow can't be tied?

A rainbow.

Why are false teeth like stars?

They come out at night.

What goes all around a pasture
but never moves?

A fence.

Why did the boy throw
butter out the window?

Because he wanted to see a butterfly!

What is H204?

Drinking.

What can you hold without touching?

Your breath.

What goes up the chimney down, but not
down the chimney up?

An umbrella.

What is big, red, and eats rocks?

A big red rock eater.

What goes all over the world but doesn't move?

The highway.

What starts with a P, ends with an E, and has a million letters in it?

Post Office.

What is always behind the times?

The back of a watch.

Why can't it rain for two days in a row?

Because there is a night in between.

What is the fiercest flower in the garden?

The tiger lily.

What goes up and down but never moves?

A flight of stairs.

How many seconds are there in a year?

twelve . . . 2nd of January, 2nd of February . . .

Which candle burns longer, a red one or a green one?

Neither, they both burn shorter.

Which is the longest rope?

Europe.

What runs but doesn't get anywhere?

A refrigerator.

What can be caught, heard but never seen?

A remark.

What kind of ship never sinks?

Friendship.

What cup can you never drink out of?

A hiccup.

What kind of star wears sunglasses?

A movie star.

What belongs to you but is used more by other people?

Your name.

What kind of cup can't hold water?

A cupcake.

When things go wrong what
can you always count on?

Your fingers.

What can you give away but also keep?

A cold.

What bet can never be won?

The alphabet.

What has two hands, no fingers,
stands still and goes?

A clock.

What is the beginning of eternity, the end of
time, the beginning of every ending?

The letter 'E'.

What can't walk but can run?

A river.

What is there more of the less you see?

Darkness.

How can you double your money?

Look at it in the mirror.

What part of a fish weighs the most?

The scales.

What's grey and can't see
well from either end?

A donkey with its eyes shut.

What is bigger when it's upside down?

The number 6.

Why don't bananas get lonely?

Because they hang around in bunches.

What's the difference between
a joke and a wise-guy?

One is funny, and one thinks he's funny.

If a woman is born in China, grows up in
Australia, goes to live in America and dies
in New Orleans, what is she?

Dead.

What has a hundred limbs but cannot walk?

A tree.

Why did the boy sit on his watch?

He wanted to be on time.

How can you tell an undertaker?

By his grave manner.

If a horse loses its tail, where
could it get another?

At a re-tail store.

What goes through water
but doesn't get wet?

A ray of light.

What do elephants play marbles with?

Old bowling balls.

Why do doctors wear masks
when operating?

*Because if they make a mistake, no one will
know who did it!*

Why is a bride always out of luck
on her wedding day?

Because she never marries the best man.

When Adam introduced himself to Eve, what three words did he use which read the same, backward and forward?

'Madam, I'm Adam.'

Why is a ladies' belt like a garbage truck?

Because it goes around and around, and gathers the waist.

When is a chair like a woman's dress?

When it's satin.

What is the difference between a hungry person and a greedy person?

One longs to eat, and the other eats too long.

On what nuts can pictures hang?

Walnuts.

What did the dentist say to the golfer?

'You've got a hole in one!'

When a boy falls into the water,
what is the first thing he does?

Gets wet.

What happened when the Eskimo girl
had a fight with her boyfriend?

She gave him the cold shoulder.

What do you call someone who doesn't
have all their fingers on one hand?

Normal. You have fingers on both hands.

Why did the girl tear the calendar?

Because she wanted to take a month off.

What did Cinderella say when her photos didn't arrive?

'Some day my prints will come.'

Why did the Invisible Man's wife
understand him so well?

Because she could see right through him.

Why can't anyone stay angry with actors?

Because they always make up.

Why did the boy laugh after his operation?

Because the doctor put him in stitches.

If everyone bought a white car,
what would we have?

A white carnation.

What is a forum?

One-um plus three-um.

What did the burglar say to the lady who
caught him stealing her silver?

'I'm at your service, ma'am.'

Why didn't the boy go to work
in the wool factory?

Because he was too young to dye.

Why did the boy put his bed
in the fireplace?

So he could sleep like a log.

When does a timid girl turn to stone?

When she becomes a little bolder (boulder)!

What ten letter word starts with gas?

A-U-T-O-M-O-B-I-L-E.

What did Santa Claus's wife say
during a thunderstorm?

'Come and look at the rain, dear.'

Why are good intentions like
people who faint?

They need carrying out.

Why were the boy's photos not ready
when he called for them?

The photographer was a late developer.

'Do these stairs take you to the third floor?'

'No, I'm afraid you'll have to walk!'

What did the mother shrimp say to her
baby when they saw a submarine?

'Don't be scared – it's only a can of people.'

Why is an island like the letter T?

Because it's in the middle of water.

Why do we dress baby girls in pink
and baby boys in blue?

Because babies can't dress themselves.

Obviously radical babies

What is higher without the head,
than with it?

A pillow.

What kind of song can you sing in the car?

A cartoon (car tune)!

How does a boat show its affection?

By hugging the shore.

What did the buffalo say to his son,
when he went away on a long trip?

'Bison.'

What do you draw without
a pencil or paper?

A window shade.

Who gets the sack every
time he goes to work?

The postman.

Why was number 10 scared?

Because 7 8 9 (seven ate nine).

What has no legs but can walk?

A pair of shoes.

What is a prickly pear?

Two hedgehogs.

What runs down the street but has no legs?

The kerb.

Why was the mother flea so sad?

Because her children were going to the dogs.

Which word if pronounced right is wrong
and if pronounced wrong is right?

Wrong.

How do you make a pair of trousers last?

Make the coat first.

What goes around the house and in the house but never touches the house?

The sun.

What is round and deep but could not be filled up by all the water in the world?

A colander.

The more you take, the more you leave behind. What am I?

Footsteps.

What is put on a table and cut but never eaten?

A pack of cards.

What trees do fortune-tellers look at?

Palms.

What is the longest word in the world?

*Smiles, because there is a mile between
the beginning and the end.*

What has eyes but cannot see?

A potato.

What starts working only when it's fired?

A rocket.

What is at the end of the world?

The letter 'D'.

What burns longer, a 10 centimetre candle or a 20 centimetre candle?

Neither, they both burn shorter.

What happened to the horse that swallowed the dollar coin?

He bucked.

What can you hold but never touch?

A conversation.

What did Tennessee?

The same thing Arkansas.

What's the centre of gravity?

The letter 'V'.

What clothes does a house wear?

Address.

Where does Friday come before
Wednesday?

In the dictionary.

What do you call a man who shaves
fifteen times a day?

A barber.

If a butcher is two metres tall and has
size eleven feet, what does he weigh?

Meat.

What's black when clean and
white when dirty?

A blackboard.

Does a death adder die if it
bites its own tongue?

Can a snail have houseguests?

If a seven-11 is open 24 hours a day, 365 days
a year, why are there locks on the doors?

If olive oil is made from olives and
peanut oil is made from peanuts,
what is baby oil made from?

Is it easier to break the long jump
world record in a leap year?

If nothing ever sticks to Teflon,
how does Teflon stick to the pan?

Do they sterilise needles for lethal injections?

What was the best thing before sliced bread?

What does a girl look for,
but hopes she'll never find?

A hole in her pantyhose.

Where can you always find a helping hand?

At the end of your arm.

What weighs more, a kilo of lead
or a kilo of feathers?

They both weigh the same.

Why is milk the fastest thing in the world?

Because it's pasteurised before you see it.

What sort of ring is always square?

A boxing ring.

What's taken before you get it?

Your picture.

What starts with an 'e', ends with an 'e'
and only has one letter in it?

An envelope!

What did the piece of wood say to the drill?

You bore me.

Which room has no door, no windows,
no floor and no roof?

A mushroom.

What washes up on very small beaches?

Microwaves.

What gets bigger and bigger as
you take more away from it?

A hole.

Why do you go to bed?

Because the bed will not come to you.

What has teeth but cannot eat?

A comb.

What goes up and does not come down?

Your age.

What question can you never answer yes to?

Are you asleep?

What is the only true cure for dandruff?

Baldness.

What was the highest mountain before
Mt Everest was discovered?

Mt Everest.

What runs across the floor without legs?

Water.

What has holes and holds water?

A sponge.

What puzzles make you angry?

Crossword puzzles.

What has four fingers and
a thumb but is not a hand?

A glove.

What flies around all day but
never goes anywhere?

A flag.

What kind of coat can you put
on only when it's wet?

A coat of paint.

What weapon was most feared by medieval
knights?

A can-opener.

Where were potatoes first found?

In the ground.

How long should a person's legs be?

Long enough to reach their feet.

When is it bad luck to be
followed by a big black cat?

When you are a little grey mouse.

What dance do hippies hate?

A square dance.

Why did the girl keep a ruler
on her newspaper?

Because she wanted to get the story straight.

Why did the girl buy a set of tools?

Everyone said she had a screw loose.

What do well-behaved young lambs
say to their mothers?

'Thank ewe!'

What can you serve, but never eat?

A tennis ball.

Three men were in a boat. It capsized but
only two got their hair wet. Why?

The third man was bald!

What's the difference between
an oak tree and a tight shoe?

*One makes acorns, the other
makes corns ache.*

What did one angel say to the other angel?

'Halo.'

What did the egg say to the whisk?

'I know when I'm beaten.'

What does every girl have that
she can always count on?

Fingers.

What do you get if you cross
a cowboy with a stew?

Hopalong Casserole.

What do you call a ship that lies on the bottom of the ocean and shakes?

A nervous wreck.

How do you make a hotdog stand?

Steal its chair.

Why was Thomas Edison able to invent the light bulb?

Because he was very bright.

What's the best way to win a race?

Run faster than everyone else.

During which battle was Lord Nelson killed?

His last one.

What was more useful than the invention of the first telephone?

The second telephone.

What did one tomato say to the
other that was behind?

'Ketchup!'

What's small, annoying and really ugly?

*I don't know but it comes when
I call my sister's name.*

What side of an apple is the left side?

The side that hasn't been eaten.

What invention allows you to
see through walls?

A window.

What are the four letters the dentist
says when a patient visits him?

ICDK (I see decay).

What's another word for tears?

Glumdrops.

Which months have 28 days?

All of them.

What's green, covered in custard and sad?

Apple grumble.

How do you make a fire with two sticks?

Make sure one of them is a match.

What did the little light bulb say to its mum?

'I wuv you watts and watts.'

Where was Solomon's temple?

On his head.

What fly has laryngitis?

A horsefly (hoarse fly).

What did one wall say to the other wall?

'I'll meet you at the corner.'

Why was the maths book sad?

Because it had too many problems.

What's the letter that ends everything?

The letter 'G'.

What did the stamp say to the envelope?

'Stick with me and we will go places.'

I have ten legs, twenty arms and
fifty-four feet. What am I?

A liar.

What did the tie say to the hat?

'You go on ahead, I'll just hang around.'

Who is scared of wolves and swears?

Little Rude Riding Hood.

What did the pencil sharpener
say to the pencil?

'Stop going in circles and get to the point!'

What do Alexander the Great and
Kermit the Frog have in common?

The same middle name!

There are three kinds of people in the world.

Those who can count. And those who can't.

Where do you find giant snails?

At the ends of their fingers.

Name three inventions that have
helped man up in the world.

The elevator, the ladder and the alarm clock.

How do you saw the sea in half?

With a sea-saw.

What's the difference between a
night-watchman and a butcher?

*One stays awake and the
other weighs a steak!*

What's easy to get into but
hard to get out of?

Trouble.

What has many rings but no fingers?

A telephone.

What do you get if you jump
into the Red Sea?

Wet.

What do you call a lazy toy?

An inaction figure.

How do you make holy water?

You burn the hell out of it.

What do all the Smiths in the
phone book have in common?

They all have phones.

Why did the bacteria cross the microscope?

To get to the other slide.

What did the little mountain
say to the big mountain?

'Hi Cliff!'

Why did the traffic light turn red?

*You would too if you had to change
in the middle of the street!*

What do bees do if they want to
catch public transport?

Wait at a buzz stop.

What is the difference between
a jeweller and a jailer?

*A jeweller sells watches and
a jailer watches cells.*

What did one rain drop say to the other?

'Two's company, three's a cloud.'

What did the penny say to the other penny?

We make perfect cents.

What did the Pacific Ocean say to the
Atlantic Ocean?

Nothing. It just waved.

Who was the smallest man in the world?

The guard who fell asleep on his watch.

What can jump higher than a house?

Anything, houses can't jump!

What sort of star is dangerous?

A shooting star.

Which of the witch's friends eats the fastest?

The goblin.

Why did the balloon burst?

Because it saw a lolly pop.

Why did the farmer plough his field with a steamroller?

He wanted to grow mashed potatoes.

What's the difference between an
elephant and a matterbaby?

What's a matterbaby?

Nothing, but thanks for asking!

What did the shirt say to the blue jeans?

'Meet you on the clothesline—
that's where I hang out!'

What did the big hand of the
clock say to the little hand?

'Got a minute?'

What kind of music does your
father like to sing?

Pop music.

What's the easiest way to find a pin in your
carpet?

Walk around in your bare feet.

What did the parents say to their
son who wanted to play drums?

'Beat it!'

What's the difference between
Santa Claus and a warm dog?

Santa wears the suit, but a dog just pants.

Where do you find baby soldiers?

In the infantry.

Can February March?

No. But April May.

What's the definition of intense?

That's where campers sleep.

What do you call a man who stands around
and makes faces all day?

A clockmaker.

Did you hear the one about the man
who went into the cloning shop?

When he came out he was beside himself!

What did the key say to the glue?

*'You wanna be in show biz kid? Stick
to me, I can open up doors for you!'*

When does B come after U?

When you take some of its honey.

What did the didgerido?

Answered the phone when the boomerang.

Where are the Andes?

At the end of your armies.

Where does a sick ship go?

To the dock.

Did I tell you the joke about the high wall?

I'd better not, you might not get over it.

What did the first mind reader say to the second mind reader?

'You're all right, how am I?'

What did one ear say to the other ear?

'Between you and me we need a haircut.'

What flowers grow under your nose?

Tulips.

What did the ear 'ear.

Only the nose knows.

Did you know that Davey Crockett
had three ears?

A right ear, a left ear and a wild frontier.

Why was the glow-worm unhappy?

Her children weren't very bright.

Why does the ocean roar?

*You would too if you had
crabs on your bottom.*

What will go up a drainpipe down
but won't go down a drainpipe up?

An umbrella.

What would you call superman
if he lost all his powers?

Man.

What has a hundred legs but can't walk?

Fifty pairs of pants.

What are the names of the small
rivers that run into the Nile?

The juve-niles.

What do you know about the Dead Sea?

Dead? I didn't even know it was sick!

Where is the English Channel?

Not sure – it's not on my TV.

Name an animal that lives in Lapland.

A reindeer.

Now name another.

Another reindeer.

What fur do we get from a tiger?

As fur as possible.

Statistics say that one in three
people is mentally ill.

So check your friends and if two of
them seem okay, you're the one . . .

What birds are found in Portugal?

Portu-geese.

Name three famous poles.

North, south and tad.

How do you make a potato puff?

Chase it around the garden.

What jam can't you eat?

A traffic jam.

If the Mounties always get their man,
what do postmen always get?

Their mail.

Why are giraffes good friends to have?

Because they stick their neck out for you.

What do you get if you cross a
worm with a baby goat?

A dirty kid.

What's the hottest letter in the alphabet?

It's 'b', because it makes oil boil!

What do you get when you cross an
orange with a squash court?

Orange squash.

What's green and short and
goes camping?

A boy sprout.

We went for a holiday last year
to a seaside town.

*It was so boring there that the tide went
out one day and didn't come back!*

What happened when there was a
fight in the fish and chip shop?

Two fish got battered.

What's the difference between a
young lady and a fresh loaf?

*One is a well-bred maid and the
other is well-made bread.*

What did the big chimney
say to the little chimney?

'You're too young to smoke.'

What did the big telephone
say to the little telephone?

'You're too young to get engaged.'

What did the power point say to the plug?

'*Socket to me.*'

What has four wheels and flies?

A garbage truck.

What helps keep your teeth together?

Toothpaste.

What is red and white?

Pink.

How do fishermen make a net?

*They make lots of holes and
tie them together with string.*

What time do most people
go to the dentist?

Tooth-hurty.

What's small and wobbly and
sits in a pram?

A jelly baby.

Why do artists make lots of money?

Because they can draw their own wages.

When do mathematicians die?

When their number is up.

What is the difference between
a bus driver and a cold?

*One knows the stops, the
other stops the nose.*

What did the ground say to the rain?

'If this keeps up, I'll be mud.'

What vegetable goes well
with jacket potatoes?

Button mushrooms.

Who steals from her grandma's house?

Littler Red Robin Hood.

What colour is a hiccup?

Burple.

Why was the broom late?

It overswept.

How do Eskimos dress?

As quickly as possible.

How do you make a Maltese cross?

Hit him on the head.

How much does Uluru (Ayers Rock) weigh?

One stone.

What's purple, 5000 years old and
400 kilometres long?

The Grape Wall of China.

When is a car not a car?

When it has turned into a driveway.

What do you do with crude oil?

Teach it some manners.

Why did the car get a puncture?

There was a fork in the road.

What do you call a man with
a bus on his head?

Dead.

How many animals did
Moses fit in the Ark?

None, it was Noah's Ark.

How did Noah steer the Ark at night?

He switched on the floodlights.

Where was Noah when the
lights went out?

In d'ark.

What did Noah say as he was
loading the animals?

'Now I herd everything.'

How do we know that Moses was sick?

God gave him tablets.

How did the Vikings send messages?

By Norse code.

Do you know where to find elephants?

Elephants don't need finding – they're so big they don't get lost.

Where are English kings and queens crowned?

On the head.

Where's Hadrian's Wall?

Around his garden.

Who invented the weekend?

*Robinson Crusoe – he had all
his work done by Friday.*

Who is the smelliest person
in the world?

King Pong.

What do traffic wardens
put on their sandwiches?

Traffic jam.

Did you hear about the
criminal contortionist?

He turned himself in.

Why was the baby pen crying?

*Because its mum was
doing a long sentence.*

Did you hear about the unlucky sailor?

First he was shipwrecked, then he was rescued – by the Titanic.

Can a match box?

No but a tin can.

Why are gloves clumsy?

Because they're all fingers and thumbs.

Why did the snowman dress up?

Because he was going to the snowball.

What happened when the bell
fell in the swimming pool?

It got wringing wet.

Why did the gangster kill his pet pig?

Because it squealed to the police.

How did the comedian pass
the time in hospital?

By telling sick jokes.

Why did the criminals
whisper in the meadow?

*Because they didn't want to
be overheard by the grass.*

When is a car like a frog?

When it is being toad.

Twenty puppies were stolen from
a pet shop. Police are warning
people to look out for anyone
selling hot dogs.

Why does the Statue of Liberty
stand in New York harbour?

Because it can't sit down.

What is green and pecks on trees?

Woody Wood Pickle.

What wears an anorak and
pecks on trees?

Woody Wood Parka.

What did the waterfall say
to the fountain?

'You're just a little squirt.'

Who's faster than a speeding
bullet and full of food?

Super Market.

Who delivers Christmas
presents to the wrong houses?

Santa Flaws.

Which song is top of the
Eskimo hit parade?

*'There's No Business
Like Snow Business.'*

What wears nine gloves,
eighteen shoes and a mask?

A baseball team.

How do you get four suits
for a couple of dollars?

Buy a pack of cards.

Why is the Mississippi
such an unusual river?

It has four eyes and can't even see.

What did one elevator say
to the other?

*'I think I'm coming down
with something.'*

What did one magnet say
to the other magnet?

'I find you very attractive.'

What did the rug say to the floor?

'Don't move, I've got you covered.'

How do prisoners call home?

On cell phones.

Why do bagpipers walk
when they play?

*They're trying to get
away from the noise.*

What's Chinese and deadly?

Chop sueycide.

Why is it impossible to die of
starvation in the desert?

*Because of the sand which is there
(sandwiches there).*

What did the dentist want?

*The tooth, the whole tooth
and nothing but the tooth.*

Why did the belt go to jail?

Because it held up a pair of pants.

Police have arrested two kids,
one for playing with fireworks,
and one for stealing a battery.
They charged one and let the
other one off.

Who were the world's shortest lovers?

Gnomeo and Juliet.

What do you get when
two prams collide?

A creche.

What are government workers
called in Spain?

Seville servants.

How do you make antifreeze?

Lock her outside in the cold.

What did the shoe say to the foot?

'You're having me on.'

Who swings through the cakeshop, yodelling?

Tarzipan.

What did one sole say to the other?

*'I think we're being followed
by a couple of heels.'*

Why did E.T. have such big eyes?

Because he saw his phone bill.

What were the gangster's final words?

*'What is that violin doing
in my violin case?'*

What's the definition of minimum?

A very small mother.

What illness do retired pilots get?

Flu.

When is a door not a door?

When it is ajar.

Where do old Volkswagens go?

To the old volks home.

Which trees are always sad?

Pine trees.

When is the cheapest time
to phone friends?

When they're not home.

How do you clean the sky?

With a skyscraper.

Why did the bungy jumper
take a vacation?

Because he was at the end of his rope.

Who was the father of the Black Prince?

Old King Coal.

Why did the Mexican push
his wife over the cliff?

Tequila.

What did the electrician's wife
say when he got home?

'Wire you insulate.'

Which bus could sail the oceans?

Columbus.

Why did Henry VIII have so many wives?

He liked to chop and change.

What did the hat say to the scarf?

'You hang around and I'll go ahead.'

When does the alphabet
only have 24 letters?

When U and I aren't there.

Why are rivers lazy?

Because they never get off their beds.

What do you call a snowman with a suntan?

A puddle.

Did Adam and Eve have a date?

No, they had an apple.

Where did Captain Cook stand
when he landed in Australia?

On his feet.

How do you use an Egyptian doorbell?

Toot-and-come-in.

How can you tell a dogwood tree?

By its bark.

Where does Tarzan buy his clothes?

At a jungle sale.

Why did Polly put the kettle on?

She didn't have anything else to wear.

Why do toadstools grow so close together?

They don't need mushroom.

Where did the king keep his armies?

Up his sleevies.

What do you call a boomerang
that doesn't come back to you?

A stick.

Where was the Declaration of
Independence signed?

At the bottom.

Why does lightning shock people?

It doesn't know how to conduct itself.

What's the easiest way to get on TV?

Sit on it.

What has four legs and doesn't walk?

A table.

What's brown, hairy and
has no legs but walks?

Dad's socks.

'Mum, why isn't my nose
twelve inches long?'

'Because then it would be a foot.'

How did the rocket lose his job?

He was fired.

Knock Knock Jokes

Knock Knock
Who's there?
Alison!
Alison who?
Alison to the radio!

Knock Knock
Who's there?
Ahmed!
Ahmed who?
Ahmed a mistake! I think I want the house next door!

Knock Knock
Who's there?
Avon!
Avon who?
Avon you to open the door!

Knock Knock
Who's there?
Avon!
Avon who?
Avon you to be my wife!

Knock Knock
Who's there?
Aida!
Aida who?
Aida whole box of cookies and now
I feel sick!

Knock Knock
Who's there?
Artichokes!
Artichokes who?
Artichokes when he eats too fast!

Knock Knock
Who's there?
Avenue!
Avenue who?
Avenue heard these jokes before?

Knock Knock
Who's there?
Avenue!
Avenue who?
Avenue got a doorbell?

Knock Knock
Who's there?
Army!
Army who?
Army and you still friends?

Knock Knock
Who's there?
Aitch!
Aitch who?
Bless you!

Knock Knock
Who's there?
Arch!
Arch who?
Bless you!

AAAARRCHOOO

Knock Knock
Who's there?
Alota!
Alota who?
Alota good this is doing me!

Knock Knock
Who's there?
Alaska!
Alaska who?
Alaska one more time. Let me in!

Knock Knock
Who's there?
Alaska!
Alaska who?
Alaska no questions! You tella no lies!

Knock Knock
Who's there?
Alf!
Alf who?
Alf all if you don't catch me!

Knock Knock
Who's there?
Alex!
Alex who?
Alexplain later, just let me in!

Knock Knock
Who's there?
Abbot!
Abbot who?
Abbot you don't know who this is!

Knock Knock
Who's there?
Accordion!
Accordion who?
Accordion to the TV, it's going to rain tomorrow!

Knock Knock
Who's there?
Amos!
Amos who?
Amosquito!

Knock Knock
Who's there?
Anna!
Anna who?
Annather mosquito!

Knock Knock
Who's there?
Adore!
Adore who?
Adore is between us, open up!

Knock Knock
Who's there?
Adore!
Adore who?
Adore is for knocking on!

Knock Knock
Who's there?
Arthur!
Arthur who?
Arthur anymore questions you have?

Knock Knock
Who's there?
Amiss!
Amiss who?
Amiss you! That's why I'm here!

Knock Knock
Who's there?
Ammonia!
Ammonia who?
Ammonia little girl who can't reach the door bell!

Knock Knock
Who's there?
Abe!
Abe who?
Abe C D E F G H!

Knock Knock
Who's there?
Abel!
Abel who?
Abel seaman!

Knock Knock
Who's there?
Attila!
Attila who?
Attila if you let me in!

Knock Knock
Who's there?
Arncha!
Arncha who?
Arncha going to let me in? It's freezing
out here!

Knock Knock
Who's there?
Arthur!
Arthur who?
Arthur anymore jelly beans in the jar?

Knock Knock
Who's there?
Abba!
Abba who?
Abba banana!

Knock Knock
Who's there?
Abbey!
Abbey who?
Abbey stung me
on the nose!

Knock Knock
Who's there?
Abbey!
Abbey who?
Abbey hive is where honey is made!

Knock Knock
Who's there?
Armageddon!
Armageddon who?
Armageddon out of here!

Knock Knock
Who's there?
Adam!
Adam who?
Adam up and tell me the total!

Knock Knock
Who's there?
Alan!
Alan who?
Alan a good cause!

Knock Knock
Who's there?
A Fred!
A Fred who?
Who's a Fred of the Big Bad Wolf?

Knock Knock
Who's there?
Abbott!
Abbott who?
Abbott time you opened this door!

Knock Knock
Who's there?
Acute!
Acute who?
Acute little boy!

Knock Knock
Who's there?
Adder!
Adder who?
Adder you get in here?

Knock Knock
Who's there?
Aesop!
Aesop who?
Aesop I saw a puddy cat!

Knock Knock
Who's there?
Albert!
Albert who?
Albert you don't know who this is?

Knock Knock
Who's there?
Ahab!
Ahab who?
Ahab to go to the toilet now! Quick,
open the door!

Knock Knock
Who's there?
Althea!
Althea who?
Althea later, alligator!

Knock Knock
Who's there?
Augusta!
Augusta who?
Augusta wind blew my hat away!

Knock Knock
Who's there?
Abyssinia!
Abyssina who?
Abyssinia when I get back!

Knock Knock
Who's there?
Adair!
Adair who?
Adair once, but
I'm bald now!

Knock Knock
Who's there?
Boo!
Boo who?
What are you crying about?

Knock Knock
Who's there?
Boo!
Boo who?
Here's a hanky, now let me in!

Knock Knock
Who's there?
Ben!
Ben who?
Ben knocking on the door all afternoon!

Knock Knock
Who's there?
Ben!
Ben who?
Ben down and look through the letter slot!

Knock Knock
Who's there?
Bab!
Bab who?
Baboons are a type of ape!

Knock Knock
Who's there?
Baby!
Baby who?
(sings) Baby, baby, baby I love you!

Knock Knock
Who's there?
Banana!
Banana who?
Banana split, so ice creamed!

Knock Knock
Who's there?
Bark!
Bark who?
Barking up the wrong tree!

Knock Knock
Who's there?
Butcher!
Butcher who?
Butcher little arms around me!

Knock Knock
Who's there?
Barry!
Barry who?
Barry the treasure where no one will find it!

Knock Knock
Who's there?
Bashful!
Bashful who?
I'm too shy to tell you!

Knock Knock
Who's there?
Bass!
Bass who?
Bass ball and softball are my favourite sports!

Knock Knock
Who's there?
Bat!
Bat who?
Bat you'll never guess!

Knock Knock
Who's there?
Bat!
Bat who?
Batman and Robin are superheroes!

Knock Knock
Who's there?
Bean!
Bean who?
Bean working too hard lately!

Knock Knock
Who's there?
Beck!
Beck who?
Beckfast is ready!

Knock Knock
Who's there?
Beet!
Beet who?
Beets me! I've forgotten my own name!

Knock Knock
Who's there?
Butcher!
Butcher who?
Butcher left leg in, butcher left leg out . . .

Knock Knock
Who's there?
Bernadette!
Bernadette who?
Bernadette my lunch! Now I'm starving!

Knock Knock
Who's there?
Beryl!
Beryl who?
Roll out the Beryl!

Knock Knock
Who's there?
Bing!
Bing who?
Bingo starts in half an hour!

Knock Knock
Who's there?
Byra!
Byra who?
Byra light of the silvery moon!

Knock Knock
Who's there?
Bjorn!
Bjorn who?
Bjorn free!

Knock Knock
Who's there?
Bolton!
Bolton who?
Bolton the door! That's why I can't get in!

Knock Knock
Who's there?
Bear!
Bear who?
Bearer of glad tidings!

Knock Knock
Who's there?
Butcher!
Butcher who?
Butcher hand on the doorknob and let me in!

Knock Knock
Who's there?
Butcher!
Butcher who?
Butcher money where your mouth is!

Knock Knock
Who's there?
Bear!
Bear who?
Bear bum!

Knock Knock
Who's there?
Betty!
Betty who?
Betty late than never!

Knock Knock
Who's there?
Betty!
Betty who?
Betty let me in or they'll be trouble!

Knock Knock
Who's there?
Bach!
Bach who?
Bach of chips!

Knock Knock
Who's there?
Back!
Back who?
Back off, I'm going to force my way in!

Knock Knock
Who's there?
Bacon!
Bacon who?
Bacon a cake for
your birthday!

Knock Knock
Who's there?
Bart!
Bart who?
Bartween you and me, I'm sick of
standing in the cold!

Knock Knock
Who's there?
Bee!
Bee who?
Bee careful!

Knock Knock
Who's there?
Beef!
Beef who?
Bee fair now!

Knock Knock
Who's there?
Butter!
Butter who?
Butter wear a coat when you come out. It's cold!

Knock Knock
Who's there?
Brie!
Brie who?
Brie me my supper!

Knock Knock
Who's there?
Bassoon!
Bassoon who?
Bassoon things will be better!

Knock Knock
Who's there?
Bea!
Bea who?
Because I'm worth it!

Knock Knock
Who's there?
Barbie!
Barbie who?
Barbie Q!

Knock Knock
Who's there?
Beezer!
Beezer who?
Beezer black and yellow and make honey!

Knock Knock
Who's there?
Ben Hur!
Ben Hur who?
Ben Hur almost an hour so let me in!

Knock Knock
Who's there?
Beth!
Beth who?
Beth wisheth, thweetie!

Knock Knock
Who's there?
Beth!
Beth who?
Bethlehem is where Jesus was born!

Knock Knock
Who's there?
Burglar!
Burglar who?
Burglars don't knock!

Knock Knock
Who's there?
Baby Owl!
Baby Owl who?
Baby Owl see you
later, maybe I won't!

Knock Knock
Who's there?
Barbara!
Barbara who?
Barbara black sheep, have you any wool ...

Knock Knock
Who's there?
Bart!
Bart who?
Bart-enders serve drinks!

Knock Knock
Who's there?
Ben!
Ben who?
Ben away a long time!

Knock Knock
Who's there?
Biafra!
Biafra who?
Biafra'id, be very afraid!

Knock Knock
Who's there?
Boxer!
Boxer who?
Boxer tricks!

Knock Knock
Who's there?
Bowl!
Bowl who?
Bowl me over!

Knock Knock
Who's there?
Bea!
Bea who?
Because I said so!

Knock Knock
Who's there?
Bean!
Bean who?
Bean to any movies lately?

Knock Knock
Who's there?
Bella!
Bella who?
Bella bottom trousers!

KnockKnock
Who's there?
Cargo!
Cargo who?
Cargo beep beep!

Knock Knock
Who's there?
Caterpillar!
Caterpillar who?
Cat-er-pillar of feline society!

Knock Knock
Who's there?
Caitlin!
Caitlin who?
Caitlin you any more money. I'm broke!

Knock Knock
Who's there?
Catch!
Catch who?
God bless you!

Knock Knock
Who's there?
C-2!
C-2 who?
C-2 it that you remember me next time!

Knock Knock
Who's there?
Cameron!
Cameron who?
Cameron film are what you need to take pictures!

Knock Knock
Who's there?
Cornflakes!
Cornflakes who?
I'll tell you tomorrow, it's a cereal!

Knock Knock
Who's there?
Celia!
Celia who?
Celia later
alligator!

Knock Knock
Who's there?
Candice!
Candice who?
Candice get any better?

Knock Knock
Who's there?
Card!
Card who?
Card you see it's me?

Knock Knock
Who's there?
Carl!
Carl who?
Carload of furniture for you!
Where do you want it?

Knock Knock
Who's there?
Chuck!
Chuck who?
Chuck if I've left my keys inside!

Knock Knock
Who's there?
Carrie!
Carrie who?
Carrie on with what you're doing!

Knock Knock
Who's there?
Carson!
Carson who?
Carsonogenic!

Knock Knock
Who's there?
Cassie!
Cassie who?
Cassie through my fringe! I think
I need a haircut!

Knock Knock
Who's there?
Cassa!
Cassa who?
Cassablanca is my favourite movie!

Knock Knock
Who's there?
Closure!
Closure who?
Closure mouth when you're eating!

Knock Knock
Who's there?
Cher!
Cher who?
Cher and share alike!

Knock Knock
Who's there?
Chicken!
Chicken who?
Chicken your pocket! My keys
might be there!

Knock Knock
Who's there?
Claire!
Claire who?
Claire the snow from your path or someone will have an accident!

Knock Knock
Who's there?
Cologne!
Cologne who?
Cologne me names won't get you anywhere!

Knock Knock
Who's there?
Cosi!
Cosi who?
Cosi had to!

Knock Knock
Who's there?
Costas!
Costas who?
Costas a fortune to make the
trip here!

Knock Knock
Who's there?
Crete!
Crete who?
Crete to be here!

Knock Knock
Who's there?
Crispin!
Crispin who?
Crispin juicy is how I like my chicken!

Knock Knock
Who's there?
Caesar!
Caesar who?
Caesar quickly, before she gets away!

Knock Knock
Who's there?
Carrie!
Carrie who?
Carrie me inside, I'm exhausted!

Knock Knock
Who's there?
Carlotta!
Carlotta who?
Carlotta trouble when it breaks down!

Knock Knock
Who's there?
Cantaloupe!
Cantaloupe who?
Cantaloupe with you tonight!

Knock Knock
Who's there?
Carmen!
Carmen who?
Carmen get it!

Knock Knock
Who's there?
Carol!
Carol who?
Carol go if you fill it with petrol!

Knock Knock
Who's there?
Cows!
Cows who?
Cows go 'moo', not 'who'!

Knock Knock
Who's there?
Cattle!
Cattle who?
Cattle always purr when you stroke it!

Knock Knock
Who's there?
Cecil!
Cecil who?
Cecil have music where ever she goes!

Knock Knock
Who's there?
Cash!
Cash who?
Are you a nut?

Knock Knock
Who's there?
Celeste!
Celeste who?
Celeste time I come round here!

Knock Knock
Who's there?
Colin!
Colin who?
Colin all cars! Colin all cars!

Knock Knock
Who's there?
Cheese!
Cheese who?
Cheese a jolly good fellow!

Knock Knock
Who's there?
Cook!
Cook who?
One o'clock!

Knock Knock
Who's there?
Curry!
Curry who?
Curry me back home please!

Knock Knock
Who's there?
Caesar!
Caesar who?
Caesar jolly good fellow!

Knock Knock
Who's there?
Canoe!
Canoe who?
Canoe come
out and play
with me?

181

Knock Knock
Who's there?
Dingo!
Dingo who?
Dingo anywhere on the weekend

Knock Knock
Who's there?
Dat!
Dat who?
Dat's all folks!

Knock Knock
Who's there?
Debate!
Debate who?
Debate goes on de hook if you want
to catch de fish!

Knock Knock
Who's there?
Dad!
Dad who?
Dad 2 and 2 to get 4!

Knock Knock
Who's there?
Dale!
Dale who?
Dale come if you ask dem!

Knock Knock
Who's there?
Data!
Data who?
Data remember!

Knock Knock
Who's there?
Deanna!
Deanna who?
Deanna-mals need feeding!

Knock Knock
Who's there?
Delores!
Delores who?
I fought Delores and Delores won!

Knock Knock
Who's there?
Dewayne!
Dewayne who?
Dewayne the bathtub before I drown!

Knock Knock
Who's there?
Denise!
Denise who?
Denise are between the waist
and the feet!

Knock Knock
Who's there?
Des!
Des who?
Des no bell! That's why I'm knocking!

Knock Knock
Who's there?
Diego!
Diego who?
Diegos before the B!

Knock Knock
Who's there?
Dish!
Dish who?
Dish is getting boring! Open the door!

Knock Knock
Who's there?
Despair!
Despair who?
Despair tyre is flat!

Knock Knock
Who's there?
Diss!
Diss who?
Diss is a recorded message! 'Knock Knock
Knock Knock Knock Knock.'

Knock Knock
Who's there?
Diss!
Diss who?
Diss is ridiculous! Let me in!

Knock Knock
Who's there?
Disguise!
Disguise who?
Disguise the limit!

Knock Knock
Who's there?
Diesel!
Diesel who?
Diesel help with your cold! Take two
every four hours!

Knock Knock
Who's there?
Doctor!
Doctor who?
That's right!

Knock Knock
Who's there?
Don!
Don who?
Don just stand there! Open the door!

Knock Knock
Who's there?
Don!
Don who?
(shouts) Don-key rides! Donkey rides!
Only five dollars a ride!

Knock Knock
Who's there?
Duncan!
Duncan who?
Duncan disorderly!

Knock Knock
Who's there?
Dishes!
Dishes who?
Dishes a very bad joke!

Knock Knock
Who's there?
Dan!
Dan who?
Dan Druff!

Knock Knock
Who's there?
Danielle!
Danielle who?
Danielle so loud, I can hear you!

Knock Knock
Who's there?
Daryl!
Daryl who?
Daryl never be another you!

Knock Knock
Who's there?
Dave!
Dave who?
Dave-andalised our house!

Knock Knock
Who's there?
Datsun!
Datsun who?
Datsun old joke!

Knock Knock
Who's there?
Doris!
Doris who?
The Doris locked so let me in!

Knock Knock
Who's there?
Dozen!
Dozen who?
Dozen anyone know who I am?

Knock Knock
Who's there?
Dish!
Dish who?
Dish is a stick-up!

Knock Knock
Who's there?
Eiffel!
Eiffel who?
Eiffel down!

Knock Knock
Who's there?
Euripedes!
Euripedes who?
Euripedes pants, Eumenides pants!

Knock Knock
Who's there?
Empty!
Empty who?
Empty V (MTV)!

Knock Knock
Who's there?
Eddie!
Eddie who?
Eddie body home?

Knock Knock
Who's there?
Eel!
Eel who?
(sings) Eel meet again, don't know where,
don't know when!

KnockKnock
Who's there?
Eamon!
Eamon who?
Eamon a really good mood!

Knock Knock
Who's there?
Eight!
Eight who?
Eight my lunch too quickly!
Now I've got a stomach ache!

Knock Knock
Who's there?
Elizabeth!
Elizabeth who?
Elizabeth of love goes a long way!

Knock Knock
Who's there?
Ears!
Ears who?
Ears some more knock knock jokes!

Knock Knock
Who's there?
Ella!
Ella who?
Ella-mentary, my dear fellow!

Knock Knock
Who's there?
Ellie!
Ellie who?
Ellie-phants never forget!

Knock Knock
Who's there?
Ellis!
Ellis who?
Ellis between K and M!

Knock Knock
Who's there?
Elsie!
Elsie who?
Elsie you down at the mall!

Knock Knock
Who's there?
Emil!
Emil who?
Emil fit for a king!

Knock Knock
Who's there?
Eugene!
Eugene who?
Eugene, me Tarzan!

Knock Knock
Who's there?
Europe!
Europe who?
Europen the door so I can come in!

Knock Knock
Who's there?
Effie!
Effie who?
Effie'd known you were coming he'd have stayed at home!

Knock Knock
Who's there?
Evan!
Evan who?
I'm Knock Knock, knocking on Evan's door!

Knock Knock
Who's there?
Eye!
Eye who?
Eye know who you are! Don't you know
who I am?

Knock Knock
Who's there?
Eliza!
Eliza who?
Eliza wake at night thinking about you!

Knock Knock
Who's there?
Evan!
Evan who?
Evan you should know who I am!

Knock Knock
Who's there?
Eileen!
Eileen who?
Eileen to the left because one leg is shorter than the other!

Knock Knock
Who's there?
Freeze!
Freeze who?
Freeze a jolly good fellow!

Knock Knock
Who's there?
Fantasy!
Fantasy who?
Fantasy a walk on the beach!

Knock Knock
Who's there?
Ferdie!
Ferdie who?
Ferdie last time open the door!

Knock Knock
Who's there?
Fanny!
Fanny who?
Fanny the way you keep asking Who's there?'

Knock Knock
Who's there?
Figs!
Figs who?
Figs the doorbell, it's been broken for ages!

Knock Knock
Who's there?
Fido!
Fido who?
Fido known you were going to be like this
I would have brought my key!

Knock Knock
Who's there?
Fitzsimon!
Fitzsimon who?
Fitzsimon better than it fits me!

Knock Knock
Who's there?
Flea!
Flea who?
Flea thirty is when I've got to be home!

Knock Knock
Who's there?
Fly!
Fly who?
Fly away Peter, fly away Paul!

Knock Knock
Who's there?
Foster!
Foster who?
Foster than a speeding bullet!

Knock Knock
Who's there?
Francis!
Francis who?
Francis is the home of the Eiffel Tower!

Knock Knock
Who's there?
Frank!
Frank who?
Frankly my dear, I
don't give a damn!

Knock Knock
Who's there?
Felix!
Felix who?
Felix my ice-cream
I'll lick his!

Knock Knock
Who's there?
Fang!
Fang who?
Fangs for opening the door!

Knock Knock
Who's there?
Fred!
Fred who?
I'm a Fred of the dark!

Knock Knock
Who's there?
Fozzie!
Fozzie who?
Fozzie hundredth time, my name is Nick!

Knock Knock
Who's there?
Gotter!
Gotter who?
Gotter go to the toilet!

Knock Knock
Who's there?
Gladys!
Gladys who?
Gladys Saturday aren't you?

Knock Knock
Who's there?
German border patrol
German border patrol who?
Ve vill ask ze questions!

Knock Knock
Who's there?
Gable!
Gable who?
Gable to leap tall buildings in a single bound!

Knock Knock
Who's there?
Galahad!
Galahad who?
Galahad a sore leg, so he couldn't come!

Knock Knock
Who's there?
Gary!
Gary who?
Gary on smiling!

Knock Knock

Who's there?

Genoa!

Genoa who?

Genoa good place to have a
meal around here?

Knock Knock

Who's there?

Germaine!

Germaine who?

Germaine you don't recognise me?

Knock Knock

Who's there?

Gene!

Gene who?

Genealogy is the study of family trees!

Knock Knock
Who's there?
Goose!
Goose who?
Goosey Goosey Gander!

Knock Knock
Who's there?
Gopher!
Gopher who?
Gopher help, I've been tied up!

Knock Knock
Who's there?
Gorilla!
Gorilla who?
Gorilla cheese sandwich for me, please!

Knock Knock
Who's there?
Guinea!
Guinea who?
Guinea some money so I can buy some food!

Knock Knock
Who's there?
Gus!
Gus who?
No, you guess who. I already know!

Knock Knock
Who's there?
Guthrie!
Guthrie who?
Guthrie musketeers!

Knock Knock
Who's there?
Grant!
Grant who?
Grant you three wishes!

Knock Knock
Who's there?
Gizza!
Gizza who?
Gizza kiss!

Knock Knock
Who's there?
Gwen!
Gwen who?
Gwen will I see you again?

Knock Knock
Who's there?
Galway!
Galway who?
Galway, you're annoying me!

Knock Knock
Who's there?
Germany!
Germany who?
Germany people knock on your door?

Knock Knock
Who's there?
Harley!
Harley who?
Harley ever see you anymore!

Knock Knock
Who's there?
Howard!
Howard who?
Howard I know?

Knock Knock
Who's there?
Hacienda!
Hacienda who?
Hacienda the story! It's bedtime now!

Knock Knock
Who's there?
Haden!
Haden who?
Haden seek!

Knock Knock
Who's there?
Hair!
Hair who?
I'm hair to stay!

Knock Knock
Who's there?
Halibut!
Halibut who?
Halibut letting me in!

Knock Knock
Who's there?
Hal!
Hal who?
Hello to you too!

Knock Knock
Who's there?
Hal!
Hal who?
Hallelujah!

Knock Knock
Who's there?
Haley!
Haley who?
Haley-ions come from outer space!

Knock Knock
Who's there?
Hammond!
Hammond who?
Hammond eggs for breakfast please!

Knock Knock
Who's there?
Hans!
Hans who?
Hans are on the end of your arms!

Knock Knock
Who's there?
Harlow!
Harlow who?
Harlow Dolly!

Knock Knock
Who's there?
Harmony!
Harmony who?
Harmony electricians does it take
to change a lightbulb?

Knock Knock
Who's there?
Harry!
Harry who?
Harry up, you're late for dinner!

Knock Knock
Who's there?
Havana!
Havana who?
Havana great time!

Knock Knock
Who's there?
Havalock!
Havalock who?
Havalock put on your door!

Knock Knock
Who's there?
Heidi!
Heidi who?
Heidi ho!

Knock Knock
Who's there?
Hester!
Hester who?
Hester la vista!

Knock Knock
Who's there?
Hey!
Hey who?
Hey ho, hey ho, it's off to work we go!

Knock Knock
Who's there?
Hijack!
Hijack who?
Hi jack! Where's Jill?

Knock Knock
Who's there?
House!
House who?
House it going?

Knock Knock
Who's there?
Holmes!
Holmes who?
Holmes sweet home!

Knock Knock
Who's there?
Howdy!
Howdy who?
Howdy do that?

Knock Knock
Who's there?
Haywood, Hugh and Harry!
Haywood, Hugh and Harry who?
Haywood, Hugh, Harry up and open
the door!

Knock Knock
Who's there?
Hugo!
Hugo who?
Hugo one way, I'll go the other!

Knock Knock
Who's there?
Hosanna!
Hosanna who?
Hosanna Claus delivers all those presents,
I'll never know!

Knock Knock
Who's there?
Ida!
Ida who?
Ida hard time getting here!

Knock Knock
Who's there?
Ike!
Ike who?
(sings) Ike could have danced all night!

Knock Knock
Who's there?
Ima!
Ima who?
Ima going to home if you don't let me in!

Knock Knock
Who's there?
Ines!
Ines who?
Ines second I'm going to turn around
and go home!

Knock Knock
Who's there?
Iran!
Iran who?
Iran ten laps
around the track
and I'm very tired
now!

Knock Knock
Who's there?
Ira!
Ira who?
Ira-te if you don't let me in!

Knock Knock
Who's there?
Ivan!
Ivan who?
No, Ivanhoe!

Knock Knock
Who's there?
Icon!
Icon who?
Icon tell you another Knock Knock joke!
Do you want me to?

Knock Knock
Who's there?
Ice-cream!
Ice-cream who?
Ice cream, you scream!

Knock Knock
Who's there?
Ice cream soda!
Ice cream soda who?
Ice cream soda neighbours wake up!

Knock Knock
Who's there?
Icy!
Icy who?
I see your underwear!

Knock Knock
Who's there?
Irish!
Irish who?
Irish I had a million dollars!

Knock Knock
Who's there ?
Irish stew!
Irish stew who?
Irish stew in the name of the law!

Knock Knock
Who's there?
Ida!
Ida who?
(sings) Ida know why I love you like I do!

Knock Knock
Who's there?
Igloo!
Igloo who?
(sings) Igloo knew Suzie like I know Suzie!

Knock Knock
Who's there?
Ivor!
Ivor who?
Ivor you let me in or I'll break the
door down!

Knock Knock!
Who's there?
Irish!
Irish who?
Irish I knew some more Knock Knock jokes

Knock Knock
Who's there?
Jamaica!
Jamaica who?
Jamaica mistake!

Knock Knock
Who's there?
Jam!
Jam who?
Jam mind, I'm trying to get out!

Knock Knock
Who's there?
James!
James who?
James people play!

Knock Knock
Who's there?
Jilly!
Jilly who?
Jilly out here, so let me in!

Knock Knock
Who's there?
Jack!
Jack who?
Jack pot! You're a winner!

Knock Knock
Who's there?
Jack!
Jack who?
Jack of all trades!

Knock Knock
Who's there?
Jasmine!
Jasmine who?
Jasmine play the saxophone, piano and trumpet!

Knock Knock
Who's there?
Jean!
Jean who?
Jean-ius! Ask me a question!

Knock Knock
Who's there?
Justin!
Justin who?
Justin time for
lunch!

Knock Knock
Who's there?
Jerry!
Jerry who?
Jerry can, even if you can't!

Knock Knock
Who's there?
Jess!
Jess who?
Jess me and my shadow!

Knock Knock
Who's there?
Jester!
Jester who?
Jester minute! I'm looking for my key!

Knock Knock
Who's there?
Jethro!
Jethro who?
Jethro a rope out the window!

Knock Knock
Who's there?
Jewell!
Jewell who?
Jewell know me when you see me!

Knock Knock
Who's there?
Joan!
Joan who?
Joan call us, we'll call you!

Knock Knock
Who's there?
Juan!
Juan who?
Juan to come out and play?

Knock Knock
Who's there?
Juan!
Juan who?
(sings) Juan two three o'clock,
four o'clock rock!

Knock Knock
Who's there?
Jaws!
Jaws who?
Jaws truly!

Knock Knock
Who's there?
Juice!
Juice who?
Juice still want to know?

Knock Knock
Who's there?
July!
July who?
July and your nose will grow!

Knock Knock
Who's there?
Juno!
Juno who?
I know who, do you know who?

Knock Knock
Who's there?
Justice!
Justice who?
Justice I thought! You won't let me in!

Knock Knock
Who's there?
Jimmy!
Jimmy who?
Jimmy a little kiss on the cheek!

Knock Knock
Who's there?
Jo!
Jo who?
Jo jump in the lake!

Knock Knock
Who's there?
Java!
Java who?
Java dollar you can lend me?

Knock Knock
Who's there?
Jeff!
Jeff who?
Jeff in one ear, can you please speak
a bit louder!

Knock Knock
Who's there?
Jim!
Jim who?
Jim mind if we
come in!

Knock Knock
Who's there?
Kenya!
Kenya who?
Kenya keep the noise down,
some of us are trying to sleep!

Knock Knock
Who's there?
Knee!
Knee who?
Knee-d you ask?

Knock Knock
Who's there?
Knock Knock
Who's there?
Knock Knock
Who's there?
I'm sorry, but Mum told me never
to speak to strangers!

Knock Knock
Who's there?
Kay!
Kay who?
Kay sera sera!

Knock Knock
Who's there?
Kanga!
Kango who?
No, kangaroo!

Knock Knock
Who's there?
Kareem!
Kareem who?
Kareem rises to the surface!

Knock Knock
Who's there?
Kendall!
Kendall who?
Kendall is Barbie's friend!

Knock Knock
Who's there?
Kent!
Kent who?
Kent you let me in?

Knock Knock
Who's there?
Ken!
Ken who?
Ken I come in, it's freezing out here!

Knock Knock
Who's there?
Kermit!
Kermit who?
Kermit a crime and you'll go to jail!

Knock Knock
Who's there?
Kim!
Kim who?
Kim too late by the look of it!

Knock Knock
Who's there?
Kipper!
Kipper who?
Kipper your hands off me!

Knock Knock
Who's there?
Lettuce!
Lettuce who?
Lett-uce in, it's cold outside!

Knock Knock
Who's there?
Lauren!
Lauren who?
Lauren order!

Knock Knock
Who's there?
Laziness!
Laziness who?
Laziness bed all day! I don't know what to do!

Knock Knock
Who's there?
Lee King!
Lee King who?
Lee King bucket!

Knock Knock
Who's there?
Luke!
Luke who?
Luke through the peephole and you'll see!

Knock Knock
Who's there?
Len!
Len who?
Len me some money!

Knock Knock
Who's there?
Leonie!
Leonie who?
Leonie one for me!

Knock Knock
Who's there?
Les!
Les who?
Les go out for dinner!

Knock Knock
Who's there?
Lillian!
Lillian who?
Lillian the garden!

Knock Knock
Who's there?
Lionel!
Lionel who?
Lionel bite you
if you don't
watch out!

Knock Knock
Who's there?
Lion!
Lion who?
Lion down is the best thing to do when
you're sick!

Knock Knock
Who's there?
Leif !
Leif who?
Leif me alone!

Knock Knock
Who's there?
Lois!
Lois who?
Lois the opposite of high!

Knock Knock
Who's there?
Lon!
Lon who?
Lon ago, in a land far, far away . . .

Knock Knock
Who's there?
Lotte!
Lotte who?
Lotte people wouldn't treat me
the way you do!

Knock Knock
Who's there?
Lucinda!
Lucinda who?
(sings) Lucinda in the sky with diamonds!

Knock Knock
Who's there?
Lucy!
Lucy who?
Lucy lastic is embarrassing!

Knock Knock
Who's there?
Lass!
Lass who?
Are you a cowboy?

Knock Knock
Who's there?
Lisa!
Lisa who?
Lisa new car, furniture or computer
equipment!

Knock Knock
Who's there?
Lena!
Lena who?
Lena little closer and I'll tell you!

Knock Knock
Who's there?
Larva!
Larva who?
I larva you!

Knock Knock
Who's there?
Liz!
Liz who?
Lizen carefully to what I have to say!

Knock Knock
Who's there?
Little old lady!
Little old lady who?
I didn't know you could yodel!

Knock Knock
Who's there?
Letter!
Letter who?
Letter in or she'll knock the door down!

Knock Knock
Who's there?
Lie!
Lie who?
Lie low until the cops leave!

Knock Knock
Who's there?
Minnie!
Minnie who?
Minnie people would like to know!

Knock Knock
Who's there?
Midas!
Midas who?
Midas well let me in!

Knock Knock!
Who's there?
Max!
Max who?
Max no difference who it is – just
open the door!

Knock Knock
Who's there?
May!
May who?
Maybe I'll tell you, maybe I won't!

Knock Knock
Who's there?
Maia!
Maia who?
Maiaunt and uncle are coming to stay!

Knock Knock
Who's there?
Malcolm!
Malcolm who?
Malcolm you won't
open the door?

Knock Knock
Who's there?
Mister!
Mister who?
Mister last train
home!

Knock Knock
Who's there?
Manny!
Manny who?
Manny are called, few are chosen!

Knock Knock
Who's there?
Mira!
Mira who?
Mira, Mira on the wall!

Knock Knock
Who's there?
Marcella!
Marcella who?
Marcella is damp and cold!

Knock Knock
Who's there?
Marie!
Marie who?
Marie the one you love!

Knock Knock
Who's there?
Martha!
Martha who?
Martha up to the top of the hill and marched them down again!

Knock Knock
Who's there?
Mary!
Mary who?
Mary Christmas and a happy new year!

Knock Knock
Who's there?
Matt!
Matt who?
Matter of fact!

Knock Knock
Who's there?
Matthew!
Matthew who?
Matthew lace has
come undone!

Knock Knock
Who's there?
Miniature!
Miniature who?
Miniature let me
in I'll tell you!

Knock Knock
Who's there?
Moira!
Moira who?
The Moria merrier!

Knock Knock
Who's there?
Maude!
Maude who?
Mauden my life's worth!

Knock Knock
Who's there?
Mayonaisse!
Mayonaisse who?
Mayonaisse are hurting!
I think I need glasses!

Knock Knock
Who's there?
Meg!
Meg who?
Meg up your own mind!

Knock Knock
Who's there?
Mickey!
Mickey who?
Mickey is stuck in the lock!

Knock Knock
Who's there?
Mike and Angelo!
Mike and Angelo who?
Mike and Angelo was a great sculptor!

Knock Knock
Who's there?
Moppet!
Moppet who?
Moppet up before someone slips!

Knock Knock
Who's there?
Mortimer!
Mortimer who?
Mortimer than meets the eyes!

Knock Knock
Who's there?
Madam!
Madam who?
Madam foot got stuck in the door!

Knock Knock
Who's there?
Major!
Major who?
Major answer a Knock Knock joke!

Knock Knock
Who's there?
Mandy!
Mandy who?
Mandy lifeboats, we're sinking!

Knock Knock
Who's there?
Mabel!
Mabel who?
Mabel doesn't work either!

Practical Jokes

Introduction

Playing practical jokes is great fun. Part of the fun comes from planning the joke and thinking about the end result. The rest of the fun comes from seeing the joke work. For a practical joke to work, there has to be a victim. The victim is the person the practical joke is played on. Some practical jokes have more than one victim. Whenever you carry out a practical joke, remember these two important rules.

- Practical jokes should never hurt anyone.

- Practical jokes should never be cruel.

This book contains some crazy practical jokes. Each joke is divided into two main sections: the Sting and the Set-up. The Sting describes what happens to the victim in the joke. When a practical joke is successfully played on someone, it is said that they have been 'stung'. The Set-up explains how to set-up and carry out the joke.

Remember when playing a practical joke that a victim often seeks revenge. Don't play practical jokes unless you are willing to take them as well.

Just one more tip before you start. Never play a practical joke on someone who you know will not take it in good spirit. Practical jokes are meant to be fun.

Warning: Some of the practical jokes in this book require adult supervision. Children should never climb a ladder, use a knife or scissors, or use a sewing needle without an adult being present. A practical joke is never worth doing if either the person carrying out the joke or the intended victim risk injury.

No Joke

This practical joke involves not playing a practical joke, which makes it a very good practical joke indeed. Does that make sense?

The Sting

It is traditional to play practical jokes on people on 1 April—April's Fool Day.

April Fool's Day is approaching. Every year, you have played a practical joke on a particular victim. This year, the victim again expects to have a practical joke played on them. You remind them that April Fool's Day is approaching and they start getting worried. On the morning of April Fool's Day, they wake up in a sweat, dreading what's going to happen today. Until midday, when April Fool's Day officially ends, they cannot relax for a second. When midday passes, they breathe a big sigh of relief because they haven't been a victim of a practical joke. At least that's what they think. The fact that you didn't play a practical joke was a joke in itself because you had them so worried.

The rabbit who wouldn't eat his carrots as a child...

What You Need

- nothing, just a victim

The Set-up

1. As April Fool's Day approaches, pick a victim who would expect you to play a joke on them.

2. Every day, remind them how many days it is until April Fool's Day.

3. Tell them that you have a really big practical joke planned for them this year.

4. The day before April Fool's Day, walk past them rubbing your hands together, as if you are getting really excited about the joke you are going to play the following day.

5. On the morning of April Fool's Day, walk past them several times and chuckle or give them a grin. This will make them feel even more uncomfortable.

6. At one minute to midday on Aprils Fool's Day, walk up to the victim and say 'April Fool'.

7. When the victim reminds you that April Fool's Day ends in one minute and that you have not played a joke on them, tell them that you've been playing the joke all morning. Explain that the joke was the fact you didn't play a joke, but you still managed to have them running scared.

The Disappearing Money

Everyone loves finding money in the street. Particularly when the money is a note. This joke gets people excited about finding money. The problem is, they can't grab hold of it.

The Sting

The victim of the joke is walking down the street. They notice a piece of paper in the middle of the footpath. It looks like money but they can't be sure from a distance. As they get closer, they realise that they're right. They can't believe their luck. They think about what they're going to buy with the money. They bend down to pick it up, and just before they grab it, it skips away. Even if they chase the money, it keeps skipping away every time they get close to it.

What You Need

- a money note

- some fishing line

- a large bush, tree, fence or wall to hide behind

The Set-up

1. Make a tiny hole in the note and thread some fishing line through it.

2. Pick a place where there is a bush, tree, fence or wall that you can hide behind. Make sure that you have a good view of the footpath, but that people walking along the footpath cannot see you.

3. When no one is coming, place the note on the footpath, then hide.

4. Hold the end of the fishing line and wait for a victim.

5. When someone bends down to pick up your note, jerk the fishing line so that the note moves away from the victim.

6. Keep doing this for as long as the person chases the note.

Set-up Tip

- You have to be very alert while you're doing this joke. Otherwise you may lose your money. Apart from running the risk of someone picking the note up before you have time to jerk the fishing line, you have to watch out for people using a foot to trap the money. If they stamp on the note before you pull the line, the note will stay under their shoe. Then you'll be the victim.

Similar Joke

- A similar joke can be done with a coin. Instead of using fishing line, use extra-strength glue to stick the coin to the footpath. Then stand back and watch people struggle to pick it free. The only problem with this joke is that you won't get your coin back.

Buzzing Balloons

If you blow up a balloon and tie a knot in the end, you have something you can kick and hit. If you blow up a balloon and don't tie a knot in the end, you have something that can whiz and buzz around a room.

The Sting

The victim of the joke is about to walk into a room. Everything seems normal and they do not suspect that they are about to have a practical joke played on them. All that changes as they turn the doorknob and open the door. As the door opens, a balloon whizzes around the room, giving the victim a nasty scare. They have no idea where the balloon came from. And if you don't tell them, they never will know.

What You Need

- a balloon

- a door and doorframe

The Set-up

1. Blow up a balloon. Do not tie a knot in the end of the balloon.

2. Place the end of the balloon between the door and the doorframe, so that the balloon is held in place and is not losing air. You may have to try various doors and doorframes before you find a suitable one.

3. Close the door and wait for your victim to open the door.

4. If you want to make a really big impact, place a few balloons in the door. The more you have, the bigger the buzz.

5. Stand back and watch the look on your victim's face as they open the door and the balloon you positioned between the door and doorframe is suddenly released. It will start to whiz about. Your victim won't be able to work out what's going on.

Similar Jokes

- Place a bucket of water on top of a slightly open door. Make sure that the bucket is fastened to something so that it tips when the door opens, but does not fall. You do not want a full bucket of water dropping on someone's head.

- Place a bag full of flour on top of a slightly open door. When the victim opens the door, the bag will fall on their head, causing a great mess. Make sure the bag is not too heavy. You don't want to knock anyone out.

- Balance a row of ping-pong balls along the top of a slightly open door. When the victim pushes the door, the balls will fall all over the place.

Holding the String

You can play this joke on one or two people. Either way, it's fun. The length of the joke depends on how long it takes before the victim realises they have been the target of a practical joker.

The Sting

The victim is walking along the footpath. You are standing nearby with a ball of string, a ruler and other measuring equipment. You are looking rather flustered. As the victim passes, you approach them and ask if they would mind holding one end of the string for a minute while you take the other end around the corner to do some measuring. The victim agrees. They stand still, holding the string. They wait for a couple of minutes and you have not returned. They are getting impatient, but they keep holding the string for a bit longer. Finally, they have had enough and they go looking for you. They turn the corner and you are nowhere to be seen.

What You Need

- a ball of string

- some measuring equipment

- a corner block

The Set-up

1. Set up your equipment on a corner block. You have to make sure that the person you ask to hold the string will not be able to see around the corner.

2. Other than the ball of string, it doesn't really matter what your other measuring

equipment is. It's only there for show, to look as if you are doing some serious measuring.

3. When your victim approaches, ask them if they could help you for a minute. Tell them that you are doing a school project and that you have to measure from the point where they are standing to another point just around the corner.

4. Pick up your measuring equipment and take the other end of the string around the corner, where the victim can no longer see you.

5. Tie the end of the string to a fence or gate. If you may want to fool another person, ask someone else to hold the end of the string and tell them that you have to check a measurement around the next corner.

6. Leave the scene. You can go home and wonder how long the victim or victims waited for, or you can hide somewhere and watch how long it takes them to realise they have been stung.

CD Swap

This joke will frustrate your victim. It is especially good to play this joke on people who are particular about the way they organise their CD collection.

The Sting

The victim goes to put on one of their favourite CDs. They turn the CD player on, take the CD out of its cover and put it in the player. They press the 'Play' button and get a shock when the music that plays is not what they expected. They take the CD out and check the label. It does not match the cover. They grab another CD from their collection and look inside. This one is also wrong. They go through their entire collection and every single CD has been swapped around.

What You Need

- the victim's CD collection

- about half an hour to do the swapping

The Set-up

1. Make sure the victim is occupied elsewhere for at least half an hour.

2. Stack the CD covers into one large pile. Do not take the CDs out of their covers yet.

3. Open the top CD cover and take the CD out. Open the second CD cover and take the CD out. Place the first CD into the second CD cover.

4. Open the third CD cover and take the CD out. Place the second CD into the third CD cover.

5. Repeat this process right to the bottom of the pile. The last CD will go in the top CD cover. (The reason for swapping the CDs in such an organised manner is to ensure that no CD is put back into its own cover.)

6. Put the CDs back where you got them from. If the victim always has their CDs in a certain order, make sure that you put them back in the same order. Otherwise they'll suspect someone has touched them.

Similar Jokes

- You can also play this joke with people's video collections and vinyl record collections.

- You can swap people's books around by swapping the dust covers on their books. To make things even worse for the victim, put some of the dust covers on upside down.

'Look, Up in the Sky'

This joke costs nothing, needs no equipment and can have many victims. That makes it a very good practical joke to play.

The Sting

A crowd of people is gathered at the bottom of a tall building. Everyone is looking up at the top of the building. Some of the people start whispering and asking each other what is going on. Over the next few minutes, the crowd grows bigger and bigger. Rumours start spreading that someone is out on the roof of the building. After about ten minutes, the crowd has become so large that it is holding up traffic. A police officer comes along and tells the crowd to move away. Eventually, the crowd does move away. Many of them watch the television news that night to see if anything dramatic happened. Of course, the incident doesn't make it to the news because nothing did happen. It was all a practical joke started by you.

What You Need

- a tall building in a busy street

- a couple of volunteers

The Set-up

1. Pick a tall building in a busy street.

2. When there are quite a few people walking past, stand at the bottom of the building and look up at the top.

3. Have one of your friends walk past and stop near you. You have to act as if you

don't know each other. Your friend should also look up.

4. Have another friend walk past and stop. Again, you should all act as if you don't know each other. One of you should point towards the top of the building and whisper something to the others.

5. By now, you should have aroused the interest of people passing by.

6. As the crowd of people grows, you and your friends should walk away and watch from somewhere else.

Similar Jokes

- If you are on a crowded beach, look at the sea and point out into the distance.

- If you are at a sporting event, stand up and look at a point several rows behind you.

- If you are in the classroom, look out of the window and point into the distance.

Cool Confetti

In this joke, confetti rains on people when they are inside a room. It can only be played on hot days when people are seeking a little cool relief. Your classroom would be a great place to play the Cool Confetti practical joke.

The Sting

A class full of children is waiting for their teacher to arrive. They are yelling loudly and running around. It is a warm day and everyone is getting a bit hot. The teacher arrives and tells everyone to be quiet and to sit in their seats. The teacher then notices that the overhead fan is not on, so the teacher switches it on. The blades of the fan slowly start to spin around. As the speed of the blades increases, confetti starts to rain down on everyone. The schoolchildren scream with delight, and the teacher can do nothing but watch as more and more colourful confetti falls from the blades and is swept throughout the room by the draught made by the fan.

What You Need

- a room with an overhead, spinning fan

- confetti

- a stepladder or desk and chair

- an adult to help

The Set-up

1. Make sure that it is a hot day. If you play this trick in the middle of winter, you'll be

waiting months before anyone turns the
fan on.

2. Pick a room where there is an overhead
    fan with wide blades.

3. Make sure the fan is turned off.

4. Climb to the top of the stepladder or place
    a chair on top of a table and carefully
    climb onto the chair.

5. Get an adult to hold the stepladder or
    chair for you. They should also make sure
    that no one walks into the room and turns
    the fan on.

6. Pour the confetti on top of the fan blades
    and spread it around.

7. Get down and hide the stepladder or put
    the table and chair back in place.

8. Wait for someone to turn the fan on, then
    watch as it starts raining confetti.

Similar Jokes

You don't have to put confetti on top of the fan blades. There are other items you can use. Here are a few suggestions:

- crumpled pieces of paper

- toy plastic flies or plastic spiders (to give people a fright)

- balloons that have been blown up just a tiny bit

Whatever you use, make sure that it won't hurt anyone when it falls from the fan.

Making an Impression

This practical joke leaves quite a mark on your victim! And sometimes the victim can walk around for ages before realising they've been stung in a practical joke.

The Sting

You and the victim are playing a game with some coins. You persuade the victim to try and stick a coin to their forehead. They do so. When they take the coin away, they are left with a dark impression of the coin. Even though everyone else can see the impression of the coin, the victim is unaware that they have been stung.

What You Need

- two coins

- a felt pen or some powder

The Set-up

1. Fill in one side of a coin with the felt pen or cover it with powder. Make-up powder is very good for this purpose.

2. Stand in front of your victim and press the coin that is not marked onto your forehead.

3. When your victim asks what you are doing, tell them that you heard on the radio that people who can stick coins to their forehead are supposed to be smarter than those who can't. Your victim will probably want to have a go, so that they can prove how smart they are.

4. Tell the victim that you'll show them exactly where the coin has to go. Then, take the coin that has the marked side and press that side firmly in the middle of the victim's forehead. Make sure the victim does not see the marks or powder.

5. Tell the victim to hold the coin firmly in place for two minutes. After two minutes, tell the victim to let go.

6. If the coin is stuck to the forehead, pull the coin off and tell them that they are obviously very intelligent.

7. If the coin falls off, grab it and put it in your pocket. Tell them that you couldn't make the coin stick either. This will make them feel better.

8. Whether the coin sticks or falls, the victim will have an impression of the coin stuck on their forehead and they will walk around without realising it.

Name That Tune

Some tunes are nice to hear once or twice. After a few hearings, they can begin to get on your nerves. After many, many hearings they start to drive you mad. This practical joke drives people mad.

The Sting

The victim is sitting in the lounge relaxing. They are reading a book and do not want to be disturbed. Suddenly, they hear a tune. They ignore it, hoping it will go away. A few minutes later, they notice the tune is still playing. Now they are having trouble concentrating on their book and they are not as relaxed as they were. After ten minutes, they get up to find where the tune is coming from. It seems to be coming from inside a cupboard. They open the cupboard door and begin to rummage through the contents. The tune is still playing. Finally, at the back of the cupboard, they discover a small device playing the tune. By now, the floor is full of stuff they have thrown out of the cupboard and they are feeling anything but relaxed.

What You Need

- a musical birthday card

- a room with a hiding place

The Set-up

1. Buy a musical birthday card.

2. Take the musical chip out of the card.

3. Pick a hiding place, such as a cupboard, in your classroom, at home, or in an office or

store. Make sure the hiding place is near where your victim sits.

4. When you know your victim is on their way, set the musical chip off and put it in the hiding place.

5. Leave the scene.

Similar Joke

- While going on a long family holiday in the car, set a musical chip off and put it down the back of a seat or somewhere else it cannot be easily reached. It will drive everyone mad (though it might drive you mad as well).

Changing Room

Have you ever had the urge to move all the furniture in your bedroom, just for a change of scenery? Well, it's much more fun if you do it to a friend's room — without them knowing.

The Sting

The victim goes to their bedroom after being away for the day. They open the bedroom door and cannot believe their eyes. Their bed is where the desk usually is, and the desk is where the bed usually is. The posters that were on the walls are now on the ceiling, and the rug from the floor is hanging over the curtain rod. The clothes that were hanging in the wardrobe have been squashed into the chest of drawers, and the socks, underpants and handkerchiefs that were in the chest of drawers are now on hangers in the wardrobe.

What You Need

- a friend's bedroom

- some friends to help you

- about half a day

- an adult

The Set-up

1. Get permission from the victim's parents to change the victim's bedroom around. (You will probably have to promise to help the victim put everything back where it was.)

2. Find out when the victim will be away from home for a few hours.

3. Make a plan at least a day before the joke. Draw a map of the victim's bedroom and work out where you are going to put everything.

4. Write down the order in which you are going to move things. This will make things much easier on the day.

5. On the day of the joke, start work as soon as the victim leaves home. You may need all the time you can get.

6. Make sure you have a few friends to help you lift and move the items around.

7. When you have finished, leave a note on the bed with a message for the victim to work out. It could be the name of a furniture-

moving service made up of the first letters of everyone who helped play the joke.

Safety Tip

- Lifting heavy objects can cause injuries. Make sure that an adult is helping you.

Leaves, Leaves, Leaves

Have you ever wondered what to do with the piles of leaves that collect under trees? Well, here's one idea that will bring a smile to your face.

The Sting

The victim wakes up in the morning and gets ready for work. They have a shower, eat breakfast and say goodbye to their family. They open the front door and go to step outside. But they can't take a single step because they are faced with the largest pile of leaves they have seen in their life. They have to push and shove the leaves out of the way before they can make their way outside. At the end of the day, when they return home, they find a huge pile of leaves again blocks their front door. This time they can't get into their house without pushing the leaves away.

What You Need

- lots and lots of leaves

- garbage bags

- a chair or stepladder

The Set-up

1. Collect as many leaves as you can from your garden. You can even offer to rake up your neighbours' gardens so you can get more leaves.

2. Pack all the leaves into garbage bags.

3. Get up early before the victim is out of bed and take the garbage bags full of leaves to the victim's house. Empty one of the bags before the front door.

4. Empty a second bag on top of the pile, and then empty a third bag and a fourth bag.

5. By now you will probably need the chair or stepladder to reach the top of the pile.

6. Hide somewhere so that you can see the reaction on the victim's face when they open the front door.

7. You could also do this joke while your victim is out during the day, or repeat it in the afternoon so they are 'stung' twice.

Set-up Tip

- Do not attempt this joke when it is windy, otherwise the leaves will just blow away before the victim comes across the pile.

Similar Joke

- If you live in an area that gets hit by snowstorms in winter, you could shovel huge piles of snow instead of leaves.

Holiday Snaps

This joke takes some organising but it is very funny. Some people use garden gnomes to play this joke, but you can use your victim's favourite toy or other item.

The Sting

The victim gets an envelope in the mail. They open it up and inside is a photograph of their favourite teddy bear at the airport. On the back of the photo is a note saying 'You never take me anywhere so I've gone on a trip by myself'. The victim races up to their room to look for their teddy bear. They can't find it anywhere. Over the next few weeks, they receive lots of photos of their teddy bear at various holiday destinations. One morning, just as they begin to wonder whether they will ever see their teddy bear again, they open the front door to find their teddy bear on the doormat. The bear is holding a note saying 'I'm back. Did you miss me?'

What You Need

- a toy or favourite item from the victim

- a camera

- envelopes

- stamps

- someone going on a holiday

The Set-up

1. Find someone who is going on a holiday and is willing to help you play this joke. If you are going on holiday, you can do it

yourself, but the victim may guess that you're playing a practical joke on them. It is best if the victim does not know the person on holiday.

2. Sneak one of the victim's favourite toys out of their room. Don't worry, they will get it back. A doll, teddy bear or other soft toy is best.

3. Give the toy to the person going on holiday.

4. Also give the person going on holiday your victim's address and a few envelopes. If the person is having a holiday within your country, you can give them the stamps they'll need. If the person is going overseas, they will have to buy the stamps themselves. You can give them some money to pay for the stamps.

5. Instruct the person going on holiday to position the toy in front of famous landmarks and take photos of the toy.

6. They should then write a message on the back of each photo and send the photos to the victim.

7. When the person returns from holiday, get the toy back and place it outside the victim's front door.

Glitter from Above

This joke requires a fair bit of setting up and testing but it's well worth the effort. It will take the victim ages to get rid of all the glitter that has fallen on them.

The Sting

The victim sits down at their desk to do a bit of homework. They get their books ready and take their pens and pencils out of their pencil case. Before starting, they decide to sharpen their pencils. They open the desk drawer where they keep their pencil sharpener.

A moment later, a pile of glitter falls from the ceiling and onto their head, their books and all over the carpet. What a mess!

What You Need

- a white handkerchief

- glitter or confetti

- fishing line

- pins or sticky tape

- a desk with a drawer

- a ladder

- a couple of hours to set up and test the joke

- an adult to help

The Set-up

1. Make a small hole in the middle of one of the edges of the handkerchief.

2. Tie one end of the fishing line to the hole.

3. Fill the handkerchief with glitter.

4. Position the ladder so that you can reach the ceiling above the victim's desk chair. Ask an adult to help you.

5. Climb the ladder and lightly pin or tape the four corners of the handkerchief to the ceiling.

6. The fishing line will be dangling from the handkerchief. Lightly tape it in a couple of places so that it sticks to the ceiling and the wall. You do not want it dangling in view.

7. Tie the free end of the fishing line to the back of the top drawer of the desk.

8. The victim opens the drawer, tugging on the fishing line. This pulls the handkerchief away from the ceiling. The glitter falls on the victim's head.

9. You will probably have to practise this a number of times to make sure that you have not attached the handkerchief too tightly to the ceiling.

The Holey Cup

Watch the frustration as your thirsty victim tries their best to quench their thirst, only to end up with the contents of their drink down the front of their shirt.

The Sting

The victim of the joke gets ready to drink something delicious. Imagine how frustrated they get when the liquid leaks out of the cup and onto their clothes before it reaches their mouth.

What You Need

- a plastic cup

- a pin

- a tasty drink

- a cloth

The Set-up

1. Use the pin to prick some holes just below the rim of the cup.

2. Tempt the victim with the offer of a tasty drink.

3. Pour the drink but make sure that the liquid remains below the pinholes.

4. Give the victim the drink.

5. Watch as the drink spurts out of the holes before it can reach the victim's mouth.

6. Use the cloth to help the victim clean themselves up.

Set-up Tips

*   Make sure that the holes in the cup are large enough for liquid to flow through but small enough so that the victim cannot see them.

*   Practise the joke with water before your victim is at your house. That way you can

make sure the holes are exactly the right size.

- Know what your victim's favourite drink is. That way they'll find your offer of a drink hard to refuse.

The Holey Straw

This practical joke is similar to the Holey Cup joke, except that it is a straw that causes the problem.

The Sting

Like the Holey Cup joke, the victim of the joke gets ready to drink something delicious. This time, their frustration comes about because they cannot suck any liquid up through their straw. No matter how hard they suck on the straw, all that happens is their face gets redder and redder.

What You Need

- a straw

- a pin

- a cup or can of tasty drink

The Set-up

1. Use the pin to prick two holes near the bottom of the straw and two more near the top of the straw. The holes should be opposite each other.

2. Give the victim the drink. It is best if it is a drink that you know they like. That way they'll find it hard to refuse.

3. Watch as they try to suck the drink up through the straw. The holes make it virtually impossible for liquid to make its way up the straw.

4. Encourage the victim to suck harder. Then enjoy the discomfort they are experiencing.

Follow-up

- You could have a second holey straw handy. Then you could tell the victim that there must be something wrong with the first straw and offer them the replacement. Watch with delight as they struggle again.

The Goldfish

Play this joke on a friend who has a goldfish. It's amazing how much a carrot can look like a goldfish.

The Sting

The victim of the joke is very proud of their goldfish. Every time you go around to their house, they show it to you. This time, as they show it to you, you mention how hungry you are. The victim goes into the kitchen to find something to eat and you follow. They have their back turned to you, but they hear you mumble with your mouth full, 'It's too late. I couldn't help myself. I was just so hungry.' They turn and scream, as they see the tail of their goldfish hanging out the end of your mouth. You take one big gulp and the tail disappears as well.

What You Need

- a carrot

- a sharp knife

- a victim with a goldfish

- an adult to help

The Set-up

1. Get a carrot.

2. Ask an adult to carefully cut the ends off the carrot. They need to carve the thick part of the carrot in the shape of a goldfish tail. (They don't have to carve the carrot into the shape of a whole goldfish, as your victim will only see the piece hanging out of your mouth.)

3. Next time you go over to the victim's house put the carved carrot into your pocket.

4. When the victim shows you their goldfish, make a comment about how hungry you are.

5. If the victim does not show you their goldfish, ask to see it, then make a comment about how hungry you are.

6. As you follow your victim into the kitchen, pull the carrot out of your pocket. Then place it in your mouth, with the tail piece hanging out.

7. Make a loud, mumbling comment about not being able to wait.

8. After you've chewed and swallowed the 'tail', say, 'Goldfish aren't nearly as bad as I thought they'd be'. Then ask, 'Have you got any more?'

Smelly House

This joke takes a while to become effective, but once it does, it stinks! And one of the best parts of this joke is that by the time the victim realises they've been 'stung', you are long gone and they have no idea who played the joke on them.

The Sting

The victim does not notice anything is wrong, at first. However, over the next few days they notice a smell in their living room. They assume that the smell will go away, but it doesn't. It just gets worse. Finally, the smell gets so bad that the victim tries to find where it's coming from. They get down on their hands and knees and, using their nose, they try to sniff it out. When they have no luck, they stand on a chair and try to sniff it out. Finally, they track the smell to the curtain behind the sofa. They look behind the curtain find some cheese, getting older, mouldier and smellier by the minute.

What You Need

- some cheese, fish or other smelly food
- an open container to put the food in

The Set-up

1. Buy some smelly cheese, a small bit of fish or some other type of smelly food. It should be fresh when you buy it, so that it does not smell straight away. You want the smell to develop slowly over a few days or even a couple of weeks. That will make it even more irritating for the victim.

2. Put the food in an open container and hide the container in a place where it cannot be easily seen. If the victim has a pet, do not leave it on the ground. Otherwise the pet will eat it and the joke will not work. Apart from behind a curtain, other good hiding places are underneath the sofa (taped to the bottom), on top of a cupboard, behind a row of books on the bookshelf, and behind a stereo system.

3. Don't let on that you can smell anything until the victim mentions it. Otherwise they may get suspicious and figure out that it was you who planted the food.

4. If you really want to make an impression, you could plant food in different places throughout the victim's house. But you'd better not let them know who did it. They might make you eat the rotten food when they've found it all.

Set-up Tip

- You don't have to plant the food in someone's house. The back of the car is a good place. So is your classroom.

Sugar and Salt

This is one of the oldest jokes around. It's an easy way to play havoc with someone's taste buds.

The Sting

The victim sits down to a nice hot cup of coffee. They've been working hard and looking forward to this drink all day. They grab the sugar container and pour sugar into their cup. They then stir the liquid and take a sip. Imagine their horror when their coffee tastes of salt instead of sugar.

What You Need

- a sugar container
- a salt container
- two saucers

The Set-up

1. Grab the salt and sugar containers at your victim's house.

2. Place the two saucers in front of you.

3. Pour the contents of the sugar container onto one saucer.

4. Pour the contents of the salt container onto the other saucer.

5. Pour the sugar from the saucer into the salt container.

6. Pour the salt from the saucer into the sugar container.

7. Put the containers back where you found them.

8. Try and be there when the victim gets a taste sensation they are not expecting.

9. This is a particularly good joke to play in a
   school cafeteria. Tell a few of your friends
   what you have done and have a laugh
   together as someone pours the wrong
   substance on their food or in their drink.

What a Mess

This joke can be played with salt, pepper and sugar containers.

The Sting

The victim sits down to have breakfast. They pour some cereal into a bowl and add their milk. They then grab the sugar container and turn it upside down so that the sugar sprinkles onto their cereal. However, as soon as the sugar container is upside down, the lid falls off and the entire contents of the container pour on top of their cereal.

What You Need

- a salt, sugar or pepper container with a screw-top lid

The Set-up

1. Take the salt, pepper or sugar container and unscrew the lid until it is right off.

2. Place the lid on top of the container. It should look as if it is sitting on the container properly, but it is really not attached at all.

3. Put the container back in place. When someone goes to use it, the lid will come right off when they turn it upside down.

The Bottomless Cup

This joke involves sugar and a sugar container. A laugh is guaranteed, as is a mess.

The Sting

The victim has just woken up and made their way to the kitchen. They are still a bit sleepy. They get the breakfast cereal out of the cupboard, the milk out of the fridge and a clean bowl and spoon from the dishwasher. They sit down at the breakfast table, pour the cereal into their bowl and add a splash of milk. They then decide to sprinkle a bit of sugar on top of the cereal. The sugar is in a plastic cup, not a container. They reach for the plastic cup and lift it towards them. The sugar pours all over the table, making a huge mess. The victim turns the cup upside down to see that it has no bottom.

What You Need

- a plastic cup (not a clear one)

- a pair of scissors

- sugar

The Set-up

1. Cut the bottom out of the plastic cup. Do not put a lid on the cup because you want the victim to see that it has sugar inside. However, you do not want a clear plastic cup, as they might notice it does not have a bottom.

2. Position the cup where the victim will find it. Once the sugar is in the cup, you will not be able to move it.

3. Pour the victim's sugar from their sugar container into the plastic cup.

4. Hide the victim's real sugar container. (Don't worry about the victim becoming suspicious that the sugar is in a different container. They will probably think that someone broke the other container or that it is dirty.)

5. Leave the room and wait for the cry when the victim picks the cup up.

6. Alternatively, you could make sure you are in the kitchen when you know the victim will use the sugar. That way you'll see the action first hand.

Similar Jokes

This practical joke is not restricted to sugar. You can cut the bottom out of any cheap plastic, cardboard or paper container. Here are a few suggestions:

- cereal packets

- bags of sugar

- bags of flour

- bags of rice

Don't cut the bottom out of a container full of liquid. The liquid will just spill out before you get to play the joke.

Jelly Juice

This joke will really frustrate anyone who is very thirsty and wants a drink of juice. No matter how much they shake the bottle, the juice just won't come out.

The Sting

The victim is very thirsty. They go to the fridge and take out a bottle of juice. They get a glass from the cupboard and unscrew the lid from the bottle. They then tip the bottle and try to pour the juice into the glass. The only problem is that the juice won't come out.

They can see the juice inside, but it just won't flow. They have a good look inside the bottle. There's nothing blocking the juice. They try once more, then give up and have a glass of water instead.

What You Need

- a bottle of juice

- an empty container

- some jelly

The Set-up

1. Take a bottle of juice.

2. Pour the juice into an empty container and keep it to drink later.

3. Following the instructions on the jelly packet, make the jelly mixture in the juice bottle. (Make sure that the colour of the jelly is the same as the colour of the juice.)

4. Hide the bottle in the back of the fridge to set.

5. When the jelly has set, put the bottle
    where the juice usually is.

6. Wait for the victim to grab the bottle, then
    walk past and enjoy the look of frustration
    on their face.

Similar Jokes

- Rather than replace the juice with jelly, you could put the bottle in the freezer and return it to the fridge when the juice has frozen. The victim won't be able to get a drink of juice this way either.

A Little Extra

One of the best things about 'A Little Extra' is that there can be a number of victims.

The Sting

The whole family is sitting down for their evening meal. It's their favourite, spaghetti bolognaise. The bowl of spaghetti is handed around and everyone serves themselves. Then the bolognaise sauce is handed around and everyone scoops some out and pours it on top of their spaghetti. It smells so good. After the cheese is added, they tuck into their meal. The first person to swallow a mouthful screams and runs to the water tap. Suddenly, a second person follows. Then a third and a fourth. The bolognaise sauce has been tampered with and is so spicy that no one can eat it.

What You Need

- a hot, spicy food additive

- a water supply where the meal is served

The Set-up

1. Get hold of a hot, spicy food additive. There may be some in your kitchen cupboard. Otherwise, you'll have to buy the additive from the store. Below are a few examples of the type of additive you can use:

   - curry powder

   - paprika

   - chilli powder

- pepper

- tabasco sauce

2. Take out the additive when someone is cooking a spaghetti sauce or a stew or casserole. These are ideal meals to add an additive to because the additive will usually blend in and not be noticed until it is tasted.

3. When the cook leaves the kitchen, sneak in and pour your additive into the food. Stir it very well, then leave the cooking implements exactly as they were when the cook left the kitchen.

4. When the dinner is served and the victims start reaching for water, do the same. That way you won't be suspected of having played the joke.

Set-up Tips

- Never play this joke if one of the possible victims is allergic to the food additive you are going to add. You do not want to make someone sick.

- The best day to play this joke is when you feel like takeaway food. When the joke takes effect, it will be too late to cook another meal, so the whole family will have to get takeaway.

- Many cooks taste their creations as they are cooking. If this is the case with your cook, then you are going to have to add the hot, spicy additive just before the meal is served.

Movie Munchies

This joke may seem a little bit revolting, but you actually don't do anything revolting at all. It's all about planting an idea in the victim's mind.

The Sting

The victim, a friend of yours, is sitting at the movies. The advertisements and trailers have just finished and the main feature is about to start. The lights go out. You offer the victim a box of Maltesers, saying you are too full to finish them. The victim accepts and eats one of them. You then say something that makes the victim think twice about eating the rest of the Maltesers. It also spoils their enjoyment of the film. What is it that you say? Read the Set-up to find out.

What You Need

- a movie theatre

- a box of Maltesers, Jaffas, Kool Mints or other round, smooth sweets

The Set-up

1. Make sure you are sitting next to the victim in the movie theatre.

2. When the lights are completely out, hand over an opened box of Maltesers, Jaffas, Kool Mints or other round, smooth sweets.

3. Tell the victim that you are too full to eat them.

4. Wait until the victim has eaten one or two of the sweets and then say to the victim,

'By the way, I put one of the sweets up my nose and then put it back in the box'.

5. You haven't really put a sweet up your nose but the victim doesn't know this. They have to decide whether to believe you or not.

6. As the victim has already eaten a couple of the sweets, they will probably feel sick thinking that one of them could have been up your nose.

7. If they decide to eat the rest of the box, they will feel very uneasy throughout the movie. It is amazing how slimy these sweets feel when you have been told that one of them has been up someone's nose.

Four and Out

This joke almost always works. It is quick and easy and makes the victim kick themselves for being made a fool of so easily.

The Sting

You tell the victim that they won't be able to give incorrect answers to four questions. Of course, the victim claims that they can easily give four incorrect answers. How easy it seems to them. They give an incorrect answer to the first question. Then they give an incorrect answer to the second question. Then they give an incorrect answer to the third question. One question to go and they are feeling very confident indeed. You throw in a comment that requires them to answer. They give a correct answer without realising that this is the fourth question.

What You Need

- nothing, except a victim

The Set-up

1. Tell your victim that you bet they can't give an incorrect answer to four questions you're going to ask them. They'll probably be so confident that you can bet them some money or get them to be your servant for a day if they fail the task.

2. Make the first question an easy one. Something like 'Are you a boy?' To give the incorrect answer, boys would answer 'No' and girls would answer 'Yes'. If they give the correct answer, then you've won your bet already.

3. Make the second question another easy one or even a silly one. Something like 'Am I your grandparent?' They should answer 'Yes', as this is the incorrect answer. If they answer 'No', you've won.

4. The third question can also be easy. Ask them what day of the week it is. If they answer with today's day, you've won. If they answer with the wrong day, they're still in the contest. They're probably also feeling very confident.

WASH DAY AT THE OCTOPUS' PLACE

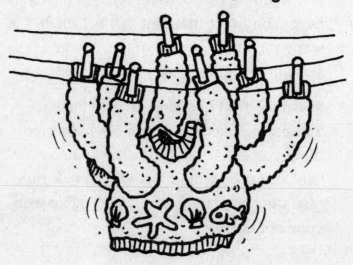

5. Now, instead of asking the fourth question like the previous ones, say 'That's three questions I've asked now, isn't it?' They will not expect that this is the fourth question and will answer 'Yes'. You then tell them that they have answered the fourth question correctly and have therefore lost the bet.

New Screensaver

Here's an opportunity to make your mark on someone else's computer, without doing any lasting damage. If your victim's confused enough, they even think their entire computer has been replaced.

The Sting

The victim of this joke leaves their computer for a few minutes to get something to eat, answer the phone, or for another reason. When they return, their normal screensaver has disappeared and been replaced by one

that has a message saying 'You have been
stung by [Your Name]' or 'I have gobbled up
your screensaver', or by a humorous image.

An owl with laryngitis

What You Need

- the victim's computer

- three minutes alone with the computer

The Set-up

1. Make sure the victim is distracted for at
   least three minutes. Perhaps arrange for
   one of your friends to ring the victim at
   a particular time, when both you and your
   victim are at the victim's house.

2. Click the Start button on the computer taskbar.

3. Move the cursor to the Settings tag.

4. Click on Control Panel. The Control Panel box should open up.

5. Click on the icon that reads Display. The Display Properties box should open up.

6. There should be a tag that reads Screen Saver. Press on this tag. It allows you to change the screensaver.

7. There is a box that contains a list of all the possible screensavers. Press on the arrow to the left of this box to bring up the choices. Select one, then press Apply.

8. If you choose Scrolling Marquee, then Settings, a box comes up allowing you to type in a message. This message will scroll across the screen when the screensaver is activated.

9. Close all the boxes so that the computer looks exactly the way it did before you touched it.

Similar Joke

You can also change the amount of time it takes for the screensaver to appear. Why not change the time to one minute, so that if the computer is idle for this short period, the screensaver will pop up. The victim will start getting very annoyed indeed.

The Dusty Phone

This joke is really only appropriate if the victim has a cord phone, with the receiver connected to the handset.

The Sting

The victim gets a phone call from a representative of the telephone company. The victim is told that in ten minutes time, the telephone lines are going to be cleared of dust. To prepare for this, the victim is told to leave the phone off the hook and put a bag over the receiver so that it collects any dust that blows out of the holes and doesn't wreck the victim's carpet.

What You Need

- the telephone number of your victim

- someone who can pose as the representative of the telephone company, without laughing and without being recognised by the victim

The Set-up

1. Make sure you know when your victim will be home alone. You want them to answer the phone.

2. Ring up (or get someone else to ring up) and introduce yourself as a representative of the telephone company in your area.

3. Tell the victim that the company is currently cleaning the telephone lines in their district. This is done by blasting air through the lines to clear any dust. In ten

minutes time, it will be the turn of the victim's line.

4. Instruct the victim to leave the phone off the hook and to put a bag over the receiver. This will stop dust ruining the victim's carpet.

5. Thank the victim, then hang up.

6. Laugh as you imagine your victim standing next to the phone, waiting for the air to be blasted through the line.

Set-up Tips

- It is very important that the person posing as the telephone company representative sound as convincing as possible. They'll need to have answers ready for any questions that the victim might ask, such as 'How long will I need to keep the bag over the phone?' and 'What sort of equipment do you use to clear the lines?'

- Make sure the person posing as the telephone company representative knows the name of the victim and refers to them by that name. Otherwise the victim may guess that it is a joke. After all, the telephone company would have their name.

Follow-up

- If you believe that the victim is going to follow your instructions, ring them back about ten minutes later and tell them that the telephone company engineers discovered a new form of dust that is invisible to the human eye. Tell them to dispose of the bag carefully, being sure not to let any of the dust escape because it could cause a massive carpet stain in forty-eight hours time.

- You could also ring back, thank the victim for their cooperation and tell them that the process will be repeated at exactly the same time over the next three days. They may not have collected any dust today, but they probably will on one of these other occasions. Tell them to set an alarm so that they do not forget to put a bag over the receiver.

Collecting Your Messages

This joke can be played on someone answering the phone or to an answering machine.

The Sting

The victim gets a phone call from someone asking for Joe Bloggs (or any other name). The victim explains that the caller must have the wrong number because Joe Bloggs does not live there. Not long after, another caller rings and asks for Joe Bloggs. This continues a number of times. The victim is getting more and more heated up. Finally, someone rings up and says, 'Hi, it's Joe Bloggs here. Have you got any messages for me?'

What You Need

- the telephone number of your victim

- a number of people who can pose as callers without being recognised by the victim

The Set-up

1. Ring up the victim and ask to speak to Joe Bloggs (or any other name other than the victim's).

2. At last an hour later, get a second person to ring up and ask to speak to Joe Bloggs (or the other name).

3. At last another hour later, get a third person to ring up and ask to speak to Joe Bloggs.

4. At last another hour later, get a fourth person to ring up and ask to speak to Joe Bloggs (or the other name).

5. When you have had as many different people as possible ring up, make another call. This time, say 'Hello, this is Joe Bloggs (or the other name). Are there any messages for me?'

Set-up Tips

- Make sure you have a lot of people willing to ring up and ask for Joe Bloggs. You do not want to repeat callers, otherwise the victim will realise someone is playing a joke on them.

- This joke can be over in a couple of hours or it can drag on for weeks. You can have your callers ring the victim one after the other, before you ring up claiming to be Joe Bloggs. Or you can arrange it so that the victim receives a call every day or two for a few weeks, before you ring up claiming to be Joe Bloggs.

- Try to get your callers to each say something different, rather than all ringing up and asking 'Is Joe Bloggs there?' For example, one could be a telemarketer trying to sell something to Joe Bloggs. Another could be Joe's mother trying to get hold of him. Yet another could be a debt collector chasing Joe because he owes them money. The more variety, the better the joke.

- Of course, if the victim turns out to have the same name as the person you are leaving messages for, then you're going to have to do some pretty quick thinking.

The cat that made off with the mouse...and the computer

Follow-up

- If you know the victim's address as well as their phone number, you could send a few letters to Joe Bloggs, after you have finished with the telephone joke. Then ring the victim up a few days later and claim to be Joe Bloggs again. Ask the victim if they have any mail for you.

Emergency Call

This joke involves leaving a message on an answering machine. It does not work if someone answers the phone. Before ringing, make sure that your victim is out and that they have an answering machine. You can play this joke on a friend without disguising who you are.

The Sting

The victim gets home and sees they have a message on their answering machine. They press the 'Play' button and hear a message that says, 'Paula, [insert the victim's name instead] are you there? It's Jill [insert your name instead]. Please answer the phone if you're home. I need your help urgently. I think there's someone in my house and they're about to . . .' The message then cuts off.

What You Need

- the telephone number of your victim

- a victim with an answering machine

The Set-up

1. Make sure you know when there is going to be no-one home at your victim's house.

2. Ring up and put on a panicky voice, as if you are in trouble.

3. Start yelling for them to answer the phone, making it seem as if the danger is getting closer.

4. Finally, gasp for breath and hang-up in mid-sentence.

Set-up Tips

- You do not want your victim to panic and call the police after hearing your call. To avoid this, leave them another message immediately after the first. In this message, just say 'Paula, it's Jill. Only joking.'

- If you know when your victim is likely to get home, you could hide near their house and sneak to their front door when they go inside. Then listen for the phone message. As soon as it finishes, knock on the door. When they answer, say 'Surprise', or dress yourself up in torn clothes and fake blood.

Similar Joke

- Rather than scare the victim, you can frustrate them by ringing up and leaving a message saying, 'Hi Paula, it's Jill. You won't believe this. I just got offered two free tickets to [the name of a concert or sports event that you know the victim would love to attend]. The problem is they have to be picked up within the next half an hour and I can't get away from what I'm doing. If you want one of the tickets, ring me up by 4.30 and I'll tell you where to pick them up. It's just around the corner from your place. If you're later than 4.30, don't bother calling. The tickets will have gone.' Of course, you have to know that your friend will be away for at least half an hour.

The Phantom Telephone

This joke doesn't involve an actual phone. However, it does involve the sound of a telephone ringing. It's designed to drive someone mad. The Phantom Telephone joke works best if the victim does not have a cordless phone.

The Sting

Your victim decides that they should do some gardening. They put on their gardening clothes and boots and go into the garden. They've been outside for a couple of minutes when they hear the telephone ringing. They take off their boots and go inside. As soon as they get in the door, the phone stops ringing. They go outside again and put their boots back on. After five minutes of gardening, they hear the telephone ringing again. They run for the door, take off their muddy boots and step inside. As soon as they do, the phone stops ringing again. This happens three or four times and your victim gets angrier and angrier each time.

What You Need

- a tape recorder

- the victim's telephone

The Set-up

1. At least a day before you are going to play the joke, set your tape recorder up next to the victim's telephone.

2. Make sure that your victim is not in the house. If they see what you are doing, they will get suspicious.

3. Using a mobile phone, ring the number of the main phone. If you do not have a mobile phone, arrange for one of your friends to ring the number at a particular time.

4. While the phone is ringing, press the 'Record' button on your tape recorder and tape the ringing.

5. On the day of the joke, set the tape recorder up near the telephone. It has to appear as if the sound is coming from the phone. However, make sure that you and the tape recorder are hidden from view in case the victim makes it into the room.

6. Turn the volume of the tape recorder right up so that the victim will hear the ringing.

7. Wait until your victim is outside or is busy somewhere in the house. Then press the 'Play' button on your tape recorder.

8. As soon as the victim gets near the phone, turn the tape recorder off.

9. Rewind the tape and get ready to play the joke again.

10. Your victim doesn't have to be gardening for this joke to work. You can wait until they are doing almost any activity. Here are a few suggestions:

- when the victim is washing the car

- when the victim is outside practising their golf swing

- when the victim is having a bath

- when the victim is doing homework

Strange Perfume

This joke is one to play on your mother, or even your big sister, just before they start getting ready for a special night out. If they don't notice that something's wrong, anyone who gets close enough to them certainly will.

The Sting

Your victim is getting ready for a special night out. They've had a bath or shower, they've dressed in a brand new outfit and they've put their make-up on. There's just one thing left. They have to put some of their new perfume on. They twist the lid off the perfume bottle and dab a little of the perfume on. Then they go out. So far they haven't realised that anything is wrong. It's only when someone comments that they smell of vinegar that they realise they've been the target of a practical joke.

What You Need

- a bottle of the victim's perfume

- some vinegar

- a clean, empty perfume container

The Set-up

1. Make sure that your mother (or big sister) is not around.

2. Unscrew the lid of their perfume bottle and pour the perfume into the clean container.

3. Fill the real perfume bottle with vinegar.

4. Screw the lid back on and put the perfume bottle back where it is normally kept.

5. Put the container with the real perfume somewhere safe. When the joke is over, the victim will want their real perfume back. Perfume is very expensive and they are not going to be very happy if you have thrown it away.

6. Wait for the victim to put their perfume on and see if they notice the switch.

Set-up Tips

- If the victim notices that their perfume has been switched, give them the real perfume back so that they can finish getting ready and go out.

- If the victim does not notice that their perfume has been switched, you may want to tell them before they leave the house. Otherwise, you may ruin their night.

- If you let the victim go out wearing the vinegar perfume, go back into their room and switch the liquids around again. To do this, pour the vinegar down the sink, rinse the perfume bottle, then pour the real perfume back in. The victim will never know why they smelt of vinegar instead of perfume.

A New Outfit

The time to play this joke is when you've spotted a great shirt, pair of pants or skirt in a shop. You can't afford to buy it yourself and you doubt your parents will buy it for you. But if this joke is successful, the chances are you're going to have that new piece of clothing the same day.

The Sting

Your mother or father starts pulling wet clothes out of the washing machine. Suddenly they stop in shock. They pull out an item of your clothing that is ripped to shreds. It must have got caught up in one of the washing machine parts. When they show it to you, you get very upset. You may even burst into tears. You tell them it was your favourite item of clothing and that nothing could replace it. Then you suddenly remember that there is one item of clothing that could possibly replace it.

What You Need

- an old item of clothing

- a pair of scissors

- a washing machine

The Set-up

1. A few days before you play this joke, wear an old item of clothing and mention to your parents how much you like it. In reality, you should choose something you are not very keen on at all.

2. Wear the item of clothing at least once more over the next day or so.

3. When you're ready to play the joke, grab a pair of scissors and make a few small cuts in the piece of clothing.

4. Make the cuts larger by ripping them with your hands. This helps disguise the neat cuts made by the scissors.

5. Wait until one of your parents has put a load of washing into the washing machine. When they have turned the machine on and walked away, sneak in and put your item of clothing into the machine.

6. When your parent shows you the torn clothing, get very upset. Try and put on an Academy Award-winning acting performance.

7. When your parent tries to cheer you, mention the item of clothing that you saw in the shop. However, do not mention it too early or they may get suspicious.

Yesterday's News

Sometimes today's news seems very similar to yesterday's news. With this joke, today's news is *exactly the same* as yesterday's news.

The Sting

Your mother or father sits down to read the newspaper over breakfast. As they eat their cereal and drink their coffee, they read the front page. Then they read the second page. So far, they're reading the latest news. They go onto the third page, then the fourth page, and so on. The further they get into the newspaper, the more they begin to feel as if they've read it all before. They check the date on the front page, but it's certainly today's newspaper. So they go back to reading. Finally, they come across a story that they are sure they've read before. They check the date on that page. It's yesterday's date. Somehow, the inside pages of the newspaper are from the day before.

What You Need

- an old newspaper (preferably from the day before)

- today's newspaper

The Set-up

1. The day before you are going to play the joke, keep the newspaper after it has been read.

2. If you get the newspaper delivered to your house, get up nice and early on the day that you are going to play the joke so that you are the first to get to the paper.

3. If someone in your house usually goes to the shop to buy the newspaper, on the day that you are going to play the joke offer to go and buy it.

4. Take all of the inside pages out of today's newspaper. You should be left with the front and back pages, as well as the second and second last pages.

5. Take the inside pages out of yesterday's newspaper and place them inside the front and back pages of today's newspaper.

6. Put the newspaper in its usual place.

7. Sit near your parent as they read the newspaper. See how long it takes them to notice that they're reading yesterday's news.

Sick Jokes

What's green, sticky and
smells like eucalyptus?

Koala vomit.

What is the difference between
broccoli and bogies?

Kids don't like to eat broccoli!

Why did Piglet look in the toilet?

He was looking for Pooh.

What's the last thing that goes through a bug's mind when he hits a car windscreen?

His bottom.

Why do little brothers chew with their mouths full?

Flies have got to live somewhere.

What do you get if you sit under a cow?

A pat on the head.

What is the soft stuff
between sharks' teeth?

Slow swimmers.

Mummy, Mummy, can I lick the bowl?

No! You'll have to flush like everyone else.

What's a sick joke?

Something that comes up in conversation.

Who is the best dancer at a monster party?

The Boogie Man!

What's the difference between
a maggot and a cockroach?

*Cockroaches crunch more
when you eat them.*

'I just got a bunch of flowers for my wife.'

'Great swap.'

What do you give a sick elephant?

A very big paper bag.

What's brown and sounds like a bell?

Dung.

Why do service stations always
lock their toilets?

They are afraid someone might clean them.

What do you do if your nose goes on strike?

Picket.

What does a boy monster do when a girl monster rolls her eyes at him?

He rolls them back to her.

Little Monster: 'I hate my teacher's guts!'

Mum Monster: 'Then just eat around them!'

Little Monster: 'Should I eat my
fries with my fingers?'

Mum Monster: 'No, you should
eat them separately!'

Mum, everyone at school
calls me a werewolf.

Shut up and comb your face.

How does a monster count to thirteen?

On his fingers.

Mother vampire to son: 'Hurry up and eat your breakfast before it clots.'

What looks like Blu-Tak, feels like Blu-Tak, tastes like Blu-Tak, but isn't Blu-Tak?

Smurf poo.

What's old, wrinkled and hangs out your jocks?

Your Grandma.

How can you tell when a moth farts?

He flies straight for a second.

How do you make a hankie dance?

Put some boogie into it.

What has two grey legs and two brown legs?

An elephant with diarrhoea.

What makes you seasick?

Your little brother's vomit.

What are hundreds and thousands?

Smartie poo.

What's another name for a snail?

A booger with a crash helmet.

What's yellow and smells of bananas?

Monkey vomit.

What's green and red and goes at 120 kph?

A frog in a blender.

What has fifty legs and can't walk?

Half a centipede.

'Daddy, can I have another
glass of water, please?'

*'Okay, but that's the twelfth one
I've given you tonight.'*

'Yes I know, but the baby's
bedroom is still on fire.'

'Can I go swimming now, Mum?'
asked the child.

*'No – there are sharks at this beach,'
said his mother.*

'Dad's swimming!'

'Yes, he's got a million dollars' life insurance.'

What's the difference between school
lunches and a pile of slugs?

School lunches are on plates.

Did you hear about the two fat
men who ran a marathon?

One ran in short bursts,
the other ran in burst shorts.

What do nudists like to eat best?

Skinless sausages.

A woman woke her husband
in the middle of the night.

*'There's a burglar in the kitchen eating the
cake I made this morning!' she said.*

'Who should I call?' asked her husband. 'The
police or an ambulance?'

My cousin spent heaps on deodorant, until
he found out people just didn't like him.

Did you hear about the two bodies
cremated at the same time?

It was a dead heat.

When the fat man was run over by
a steam roller, what was proved?

That he had lots of guts.

Boy: 'Dad there's a black cat
in the dining room!'

Dad: 'That's okay son, black cats are lucky.'

Son: 'This one is – he's eaten your dinner!'

The cruise ship passenger was feeling really seasick, when the waiter asked if she'd like some lunch.

'No thanks,' she replied. 'Just throw it over the side and save me the trouble.'

A mushroom walks into a bar and says to the bartender, 'Get me a drink!'

But the bartender refuses.

The mushrooms says, 'Why not? I'm a fun-gi!'

What's the difference between a peeping Tom and someone who's just got out of the bath?

One is rude and nosey.
The other is nude and rosey!

She's so ugly, when a wasp stings her,
it has to shut its eyes!

A man out for a walk came across a
little boy pulling his cat's tail.

'Hey you!' he shouted.
'Don't pull the cat's tail!'

'I'm not pulling,' replied the boy. 'I'm only
holding on – the cat's doing the pulling!'

There's no point in telling some people a joke
with a double meaning. They wouldn't
understand either of them!

George is the type of boy that his mother doesn't want him to hang around with.

Three guys, Shutup, Manners and Poop, drove too fast and Poop fell out of the car. Shutup went to the police station, where the policeman asked, 'What's your name?'

'Shutup,' he answered.

'Hey – where are your manners!' the policeman exclaimed.

Shutup replied, 'Outside on the road, scrapin' up Poop!'

My dad once stopped a man
ill-treating a donkey.

It was a case of brotherly love.

Three girls walked into a barber shop.
Two had blonde hair and one had green
hair. The barber asked the blondes,
'How did you get to be blonde?'

'Oh, it's natural,' they replied.

The barber asked the other girl, 'How did
your hair become green?'

*She replied, 'Now put your hand on
your nose and rub up to your hair.'*

Uncle Hubert noticed that his nephew Johnny was watching him the whole time.

'Why are you always looking at me?' he asked.

'I was just wondering when you were going to do your trick,' replied Johnny.

'What trick?' asked Uncle Hubert.

'Well, Mum says you drink like a fish . . .'

What do you get when you cross a vampire with a dwarf?

A monster which sucks blood out of people's kneecaps.

The mother monster asked her son what he was doing with a saw, and if he'd seen his brother.

'You mean my new half-brother, Mummy,' he *replied!*

What goes in pink and comes out blue?

A swimmer on a cold day!

What is the smelliest game in the world?

Ping-Pong!

A woman was facing court, charged with wounding her husband.

'You're very lucky you're not facing a murder charge – why did you stab him over a hundred times?' asked the judge.

'I didn't know how to turn off the electric carving knife,' she replied.

Roger was in a full bus when a fat lady opposite said to him, 'If you were a gentleman, you'd stand up and let someone else sit down.'

'And if you were a lady,' Roger replied, 'you'd stand up and let four people sit down!'

What do you give an elephant with diarrhoea?

Plenty of room.

Did you hear the joke about the fart?

It stinks.

Someone stole all the toilet seats from the police station. The officers have nothing to go on.

Teacher: 'How was your holiday, Penny?'

Penny: 'Great. My brother and I spent
the whole time on the beach, burying
each other in the sand.'

Teacher: 'That sounds like fun.'

Penny: 'Daddy says we can go back next year
and find him.'

What baseball position did the boy
with no arms or legs play?

Home base.

...at did the first mate see in the toilet?

The captain's log.

Why are sausages so bad mannered?

They spit in the frying pan.

What do Eskimos get from sitting
on the ice too long?

Polaroids.

Three kids were playing in a park when a genie appeared. The genie said they could have one wish each, so long as they made the wish while coming down the slide. The first kid slid down shouting, 'I want a big glass of lemonade.' The second kid slid down shouting, 'I want a chocolate milkshake.' The third kid slid down shouting, 'Weeeeee.'

What do you call a boy who eats his mother and his father?

An orphan.

What is black and white and red all over?

A nun in a blender.

What is twenty metres long
and smells of wee?

Line dancing at the old people's home.

What has four legs and an arm?

A happy lion.

What's green and slimy and
hangs from trees?

Giraffe boogie.

What do you get if you cross an elephant
with a box of laxatives?

Out of the way.

What's green, has two legs and sits
on the end of your finger?

The boogieman.

What's Mozart up to now?

Decomposing.

What's thick and black and picks its nose?

Crude oil.

What's the difference between an oral thermometer and a rectal thermometer?

The taste.

Where do lepers shop?

At the secondhand store.

Why did the boy take his own toilet
paper to the birthday party?

Because he was a party pooper.

Why do farts smell?

*So that blind people can appreciate
them as well.*

What do you find up a clean nose?

Fingerprints.

Why don't elephants pick their nose?

*Because they don't know what to do
with a 20 kilogram boogie.*

Why was the sailor buried at sea?

Because he was dead.

Woman 1: 'Your son is terribly spoiled.'

Woman 2: *'How dare you. He's not*
spoiled at all.'

Woman 1: 'Yes he is. He just got hit by a bus.'

What's invisible and smells of carrots?

Bunny farts!!

Why do gorillas have big nostrils?

Because they have big fingers.

Why did the toilet paper roll down the hill?

To get to the bottom.

Why did the surfer stop surfing?

Because the sea weed.

What is a cannibal's favourite soup?

One with a lot of body.

First Cannibal: 'My girlfriend's
a tough old bird.'

*Second Cannibal: 'You should have left
her in the oven for another half hour.'*

First Cannibal: 'Who was that girl
I saw you with last night?'

*Second Cannibal: 'That was no girl,
that was my dinner.'*

Cannibal 1: 'How do you make
an explorer stew?'

Cannibal 2: 'Keep him waiting a few hours.'

Did you hear about the cannibal who
gnawed a bone for hours on end?

When he stood up, he fell over.

How can you help a hungry cannibal?

Give him a hand.

Mr Cannibal: 'I've brought a friend
home for dinner.'

Mrs Cannibal: 'But I've already made a stew.'

Two cannibals were having lunch.

'Your girlfriend makes a great soup,'
said one to the other.

'Yes!' agreed the first. 'But I'm
going to miss her!'

What did the cannibal say to the explorer?

'Nice to meat you.'

What did the cannibal say when he saw his wife chopping up a python and a pygmy?

'Yum, snake and pygmy pie.'

What did the cannibal say when he saw Dr Livingstone?

'Dr Livingstone, I consume.'

What did the cannibal say when he was full?

'I couldn't eat another mortal.'

What do the guests do at a
cannibal wedding?

Toast the bride and groom.

What do vegetarian cannibals eat?

Swedes.

What does a cannibal say when a
bus load of tourists drives past?

'Smorgasbord.'

What's the favourite game at a
cannibal's birthday party?

Swallow the leader.

What was the cannibal called,
who ate her father's sister?

An aunt-eater!

Where do cannibals work?

At head office.

Why did the cannibal eat the missionary?

Because he'd developed
a taste for Christianity.

Why did the cannibal kidnap the tourist?

He wanted take-away.

Why did the cannibal live on his own?

He'd had his fill of other people.

Why don't cannibals eat
weather forecasters?

Because they give them wind.

Mummy, Mummy, I don't want
to go to New Zealand.

Shut up and keep swimming.

When the cannibal crossed the Pacific on a cruise ship, he told the waiter to take the menu away and bring him the passenger list!

Mummy, Mummy, Dad has been run over by a steamroller.

Shut up and slide him under the door.

Mummy, Mummy, Daddy's on fire.

Hurry up and get the marshmallows.

Mummy, Mummy, what's a vampire?

Shut up and eat your soup before it clots.

Mummy, Mummy, why do I keep
going round in circles?

*Shut up or I'll nail your
other foot to the floor.*

Mummy, Mummy, are you
sure you bake bread this way?

Shut up and get back in.
I can't close the oven door.

Mummy, Mummy, can I play with Rover?

We've already dug him up
three times this week.

Mummy, Mummy, my head hurts.

Shut up and get away from the dart board.

Mummy, Mummy, Dad's going out.

*Shut up and throw some
more petrol on him.*

Mummy, Mummy, Daddy just
put Rover down.

I'm sure he had a good reason for it.

But he promised I could do it.

Mummy, Mummy, Daddy's hammering
on the roof again.

Shut up and drive a bit faster.

Mummy, Mummy, I can't
find the dog's food.

Shut up and eat your stew.

Mummy, Mummy, I feel like a yo-yo.

Shut up and sit down . . .
and down . . . and down . . .

Mummy, Mummy, I'm 16 years old. Don't
you think I'm old enough to wear a bra now?

Shut up, George.

Mummy, Mummy, I hate my brother's guts.

Shut up and eat what's on your plate.

Mummy, Mummy, sis has got a bruise.

Shut up and eat around it.

Mummy, Mummy, what are
you doing with that ax . . .

Mummy, Mummy, when are we going to
have Grandma for dinner?

*Shut up. We haven't finished
eating your father yet.*

Mummy, Mummy, I've just
chopped my foot off.

*Then hop out of the kitchen,
I've just mopped the floor.*

Mummy, Mummy, why are we
pushing the car off the cliff?

Shut up or you'll wake your father.

Mummy, Mummy, why can't we give
Grandma a proper burial?

Shut up and keep flushing.

Mummy, Mummy, why is
Dad running in zig zags?

Shut up and keep shooting.

Mummy, Mummy, why can't we
buy a garbage disposal unit?

Shut up and keep chewing.

Doctor, Doctor, what is the best
way to avoid biting insects?

Don't bite any.

Doctor, Doctor, I feel like a tennis racket.

You must be too highly strung.

Doctor, Doctor, my nose is running.

You'd better tie it up then.

Doctor, Doctor, I'm afraid of the dark.

Then leave the light on.

Doctor, Doctor, I keep stealing things.

Take one of these pills and if that doesn't work, bring me back a computer.

Doctor, Doctor, I feel like a pair of socks.

Well I'll be darned.

Doctor, Doctor, I have a hoarse throat.

The resemblance doesn't end there.

Doctor, Doctor, I keep thinking I'm a yo-yo.

How are you feeling?

Oh, up and down.

Doctor, Doctor, how can I stop
my nose from running?

Stick your foot out and trip it up.

Doctor, Doctor, people keep
disagreeing with me.

No they don't.

Doctor, Doctor, I'm at death's door.

Don't worry, I'll pull you through.

Doctor, Doctor, my stomach is sore.

Stop your belly aching.

Doctor, Doctor, I'm having trouble breathing.

I'll put a stop to that.

Doctor, Doctor, I keep thinking
I'm a doorknob.

Now don't fly off the handle.

Doctor, Doctor, I'm a wrestler
and I feel awful.

Get a grip on yourself then.

Doctor, Doctor, I think I'm a video.

I thought I'd seen you before.

Doctor, Doctor, I feel like a cricket ball.

How's that?

Oh no, not you too!

Doctor, Doctor, everyone hates me.

*Don't be stupid, not everyone
has met you yet.*

Doctor, Doctor, I'm suffering
from hallucinations.

I'm sure you are only imagining it.

Doctor, Doctor, will you treat me?

No, you'll have to pay like everybody else.

Doctor, Doctor I keep thinking I'm a $ bill.

Go shopping, the change will do you good.

Doctor, Doctor, I swallowed a spoon.

Well try to relax and don't stir.

Doctor, Doctor, I swallowed a roll of film.

Don't worry, nothing will develop.

Doctor, Doctor, nobody ever listens to me.

Next!

Doctor, Doctor, I'm so ugly what
can I do about it?

Hire yourself out for Halloween parties.

Doctor, Doctor, I feel like a bell.

*Well, take these and if they
don't work, give me a ring.*

Doctor, Doctor, I'm as sick as a dog.

Well, I can't help you because I'm not a vet.

Doctor, Doctor, my eyesight is getting worse.

You're absolutely right, this is a Post Office.

Doctor, Doctor, the first thirty minutes I'm up every morning I feel dizzy, what should I do?

Get up half an hour later.

Doctor, Doctor, what does this
X-Ray of my head show?

Unfortunately nothing.

Doctor, Doctor, this ointment you gave
me makes my arm smart!

Try putting some on your head.

Doctor, Doctor, something is
preying on my mind!

Don't worry, it will probably starve to death.

Doctor, Doctor, I feel like a set of curtains.

Well, pull yourself together.

Doctor, Doctor, I feel run down.

*You should be more careful
crossing the road then.*

Doctor, Doctor, I accidentally ate my doona!

Don't be so down in the mouth.

Doctor, Doctor, I have a ringing in my ears!

Well, answer it.

Doctor, Doctor, every time I stand up I see visions of Mickey Mouse and Pluto and every time I sit down I see Donald Duck!

How long have you been having these Disney spells?

Doctor, Doctor, it hurts when I do this!

Well, don't do that.

Doctor, Doctor, my leg hurts, what can I do?

Limp.

Doctor, Doctor, I snore so loudly
I wake myself up!

Try sleeping in another room.

Doctor, Doctor, everyone thinks I'm a liar.

I don't believe you.

Doctor, Doctor, I have yellow teeth,
what should I do?

Wear a brown tie.

Doctor, Doctor I feel like a dog.

Then go see a vet!

Doctor, Doctor, I have a pain in the eye
every time I drink hot chocolate.

*Take the spoon out of your mug
before you drink.*

Doctor, Doctor, I only have seconds to live!

Just a minute!

Doctor, Doctor, can you help me out?

Certainly – which way did you come in?

Doctor, Doctor, I dreamed that
I ate a large marshmallow!

Did you wake up without a pillow?

Doctor, Doctor, my brother
thinks he's a chicken.

How long has this been going on?

About six months.

Why didn't you bring him here earlier?

We needed the eggs.

Doctor, Doctor, my sister
thinks she's a squirrel.

Sounds like a nut case to me.

Doctor, Doctor, I think I'm getting shorter!

You'll just have to be a little patient.

Doctor Doctor, I keep thinking I'm a dog.

How long has this been going on?

Ever since I was a pup.

Doctor, Doctor, did you hear about
the boy who swallowed a coin?

No? Well, there's no change yet!

Doctor, Doctor, my son swallowed a pen,
what should I do?

Use a pencil instead!

Doctor, Doctor, my wooden leg
is giving me a lot of pain.

Why's that?

My wife keeps hitting me over
the head with it!

Doctor, Doctor, my hair is falling out, can you give me something to keep it in?

Yes, a paper bag.

Doctor, Doctor, I keep thinking I'm a billiard ball.

Well, get back in the queue.

Doctor, Doctor, I've been turned into a hare!

Stop rabbiting on about it.

Doctor, Doctor, I keep thinking I'm a dog.

*Well, get up on this couch
and I'll examine you.*

I can't, I'm not allowed on the furniture.

Doctor, Doctor, my little boy swallowed
a bullet, what should I do?

Well for a start, don't point him at me.

Doctor, Doctor, I feel like a window.

Where's the pane?

Doctor, Doctor, I feel like a piano.

Wait a moment while I make some notes.

Doctor, Doctor will my measles
be better by next Monday?

I don't want to make any rash promises.

Doctor, Doctor, I keep thinking
I'm a fruitcake.

What's got into you?

Flour, raisins and cherries.

Doctor, Doctor, my wife thinks I'm
crazy because I like sausages.

That's ridiculous. I like sausages too.

Good, you should come round and see
my collection some time. I've got
hundreds of them.

Doctor, Doctor, I keep hearing
a ringing in my ears.

Where else did you expect to hear it?

Doctor, Doctor, what's good
for biting fingernails?

Very sharp teeth.

Doctor, Doctor, I have a carrot
growing out of my ear.

Amazing! How could that have happened?

I don't understand it –
I planted cabbages in there!

Doctor, Doctor, I've spent so long at my
computer that I now see double.

Well, walk around with one eye shut.

Doctor, Doctor, can you give me anything for excessive wind?

Sure, here's a kite.

Doctor, Doctor, can I have a bottle of aspirin and a pot of glue?

Why?

Because I've got a splitting headache!

Doctor, Doctor, my little brother thinks he's a computer.

Well, bring him in so I can cure him.

I can't, I need to use him to finish my homework!

Doctor, Doctor, should I surf the Internet
on an empty stomach?

No, you should do it on a computer.

Doctor, Doctor, my girlfriend
thinks she's a duck.

*You'd better bring her
in to see me right away.*

I can't – she's already
flown south for the winter.

Doctor, Doctor, I think
I've been bitten by a vampire.

Drink this glass of water.

Will it make me better?

No, but I'll be able to see if your neck leaks!

Doctor, Doctor, I think I'm a bell.

*Take these, and if they don't help,
give me a ring!*

Doctor, Doctor, the pain is still there.

*I can't find a cause for the pain,
though I think it's due to drinking.*

In that case, I'll come back
when you're sober.

Doctor, Doctor, I have a sore throat.

*Pull your pants down and put your
backside against the window.*

What's that got to do with my sore throat?

Nothing. I just hate my neighbours.

Doctor, Doctor, I was playing a
kazoo and I swallowed it.

Lucky you weren't playing the piano.

Doctor, Doctor, I think I'm a bridge.

What's come over you?

Oh, two cars, a large truck and a bus.

Doctor, Doctor, can I have a second opinion?

Of course, come back tomorrow.

Doctor, Doctor, when I press with my
finger here . . . it hurts, and here . . .
it hurts, and here . . .
and here! What do you
think is wrong with me?

Your finger's broken.

Doctor, Doctor, you have to help me out!

*That's easily done, which way
did you come in?*

Doctor, Doctor, I keep thinking I'm God.

When did this start?

After I created the sun, then the earth . . .

Doctor, Doctor, have you
taken my temperature?

No. Is it missing?

Doctor, Doctor, I feel like a spoon!

Well, sit down and don't stir!

Doctor, Doctor, I keep thinking I'm a joke.

Don't make me laugh.

Doctor, Doctor, I think I need glasses.

*You certainly do – you've just
walked into a restaurant!*

Doctor, Doctor, I've just swallowed a pen.

Well, sit down and write your name!

Doctor, Doctor, I feel like a dog.

Sit!

Doctor, Doctor, I feel like an apple.

We must get to the core of this!

Doctor, Doctor, I feel like a sheep.

That's baaaaaaaaaad!

Doctor, Doctor, I'm becoming invisible.

Yes, I can see you're not all there!

Doctor, Doctor, will this ointment
clear up my spots?

I never make rash promises!

Doctor, Doctor, everyone keeps
throwing me in the garbage.

Don't talk rubbish!

Doctor, Doctor, I'm turning into a dustbin.

Don't talk such rubbish.

Doctor, Doctor, I'm boiling up!

Just simmer down!

Doctor, Doctor, I feel like a needle.

I see your point!

Doctor, Doctor, how can
I cure my sleepwalking?

Sprinkle tin-tacks on your bedroom floor!

Doctor, Doctor, I feel like a racehorse.

Take one of these every four laps!

Doctor, Doctor, I feel like a bee.

Buzz off, I'm busy!

Doctor, Doctor, I'm a burglar!

Have you taken anything for it?

Doctor, Doctor, I keep seeing
an insect spinning.

*Don't worry, it's just a bug
that's going around.*

Doctor, Doctor, I need some
acetylsalicylic acid.

You mean aspirin?

That's it. I can never remember that word.

Doctor, Doctor, I feel like an apple.

Well don't worry, I won't bite.

Doctor, Doctor, my tongue tingles when
I touch it to an unsalted peanut wrapped
in used toaster oven aluminium foil.
What's wrong with me?

You have far too much free time.

Doctor, Doctor, I tend to flush a lot.

Don't worry, it's just a chain reaction.

Doctor, Doctor, everyone thinks I'm a liar.

Well, that's hard to believe!

Doctor, Doctor, I think I'm a python.

*You can't get round me
just like that, you know!*

Doctor, Doctor, I think I'm a moth.

So why did you come around then?

Well, I saw this light at the window . . .

Doctor, Doctor, I keep thinking I'm a spider.

What a web of lies!

Doctor, Doctor, I think I'm a snail.

*Don't worry, we'll soon have
you out of your shell.*

Doctor, Doctor, I think I'm an adder.

*Great, can you help me with
my accounts then please?*

Doctor, Doctor, I keep painting myself gold.

Don't worry, it's just a gilt complex.

Doctor, Doctor, my baby looks
just like his father.

Never mind – just as long as he's healthy.

Doctor, Doctor, everyone keeps ignoring me.

Next please!

Doctor, Doctor, I keep thinking
I'm a computer.

*My goodness, you'd better come to my
surgery right away!*

I can't, my power cable won't reach that far!

Doctor, Doctor, I don't think I'm a computer
any more. Now I think I'm a desk.

You're just letting things get on top of you.

Doctor, Doctor, I keep thinking
there's two of me.

One at a time please!

Doctor, Doctor, some days I feel like a tee-pee and other days I feel like a wigwam.

You're too tents!

Doctor, Doctor, my little boy has just swallowed a roll of film.

Hmmm. Let's hope nothing develops!

Doctor, Doctor, I feel like a pack of cards.

I'll deal with you later!

Doctor, Doctor, how much to have
this splinter pulled out?

Seventy dollars.

Seventy dollars for just a
couple of minutes' work?

I can pull it out very slowly if you like.

Doctor, Doctor, I snore so loud that
I keep myself awake.

Sleep in another room, then.

Doctor, Doctor, I think I'm a yo-yo.

You're stringing me along!

Doctor, Doctor, I keep thinking
I'm a vampire.

Necks, please!

Doctor, Doctor, I swallowed a bone.

Are you choking?

No, I really did!

Doctor, Doctor, I dream there are zombies
under my bed. What can I do?

Saw the legs off your bed.

Doctor, Doctor, I think I'm a woodworm.

How boring for you!

Doctor, Doctor, I think I'm an electric eel.

That's shocking!

Doctor, Doctor, I think I'm a nit.

Will you get out of my hair?

Doctor, Doctor, I keep thinking
I'm a mosquito.

Go away, sucker!

Doctor, Doctor, I've broken
my arm in two places.

Well, don't go back there again.

Doctor, Doctor, I think I'm a butterfly.

*Will you say what you mean
and stop flitting about!*

Doctor, Doctor, I think I'm a frog.

What's wrong with that?

I think I'm going to croak!

Doctor, Doctor, I think I'm a caterpillar.

Don't worry, you'll soon change.

Doctor, Doctor, I think I'm a snake,
about to shed its skin.

*Why don't you go behind the screen and slip
into something more comfortable, then!*

Doctor, Doctor, these pills you
gave me for B.O. . .

What's wrong with them?

They keep slipping out from under my arms!

Doctor, Doctor, my husband
smells like a fish.

Poor sole!

Doctor, Doctor, my sister thinks she's a lift.

Well, tell her to come in.

I can't, she doesn't stop at this floor!

Doctor, Doctor, I think I'm a moth.

Get out of the way, you're in my light!

Doctor, Doctor, how long have I got?

Ten.

Ten what? Ten months? Ten weeks?

10, 9, 8, 7 . . .

Doctor, Doctor, how was my check up?

Perfect. You'll live to be 80.

But I am 80.

In that case, it's been nice knowing you.

Doctor, Doctor, have you got
something for a migraine?

*Take this hammer and hit
yourself on the head.*

Doctor, Doctor, I ate some oysters
and now I'm feeling sick.

Were they fresh?

How can you tell?

You open the shell and have a look.

You're not supposed to eat the shell?

Doctor, Doctor, I came as quick as
I could. What's the problem?

*Your lab results are back and you've
only got 24 hours to live.*

That's terrible.

*There's worse. I've been trying
to call you since yesterday.*

Doctor, Doctor, I get very nervous and
frightened during driving tests.

Don't worry, you'll pass eventually.

But I'm the examiner!

Doctor, Doctor, I can't feel my legs.

That's because we had to amputate your arms.

Doctor, Doctor, I feel like a bird.

I'll tweet you in a minute.

Doctor, Doctor, I feel like a strawberry.

I can see you're in a bit of a jam.

Doctor, Doctor, I think I'm a rubber band.

Why don't you stretch yourself out on the couch there, and tell me all about it?

Doctor, Doctor, I keep seeing double.

Please sit on the couch.

Which one?

Doctor, Doctor, I keep seeing green aliens with two heads and four legs.

Have you seen a psychiatrist?

No, just green aliens with two heads and four legs.

Doctor, Doctor, I keep thinking I'm a bee.

Buzz off, I'm busy.

Doctor, Doctor, my wife keeps beating me.

Oh dear. How often?

Every time we play Scrabble.

Doctor, Doctor, I need something
for my temper.

Just wait 'til you get the bill.

Doctor, Doctor, I swallowed
a whole cantaloupe.

You're just feeling melon-choly.

Doctor, Doctor, I feel like a pair of curtains.

Oh, pull yourself together!

490

Doctor, Doctor, I think I'm a clock.

You're winding me up.

Doctor, Doctor, I think I'm invisible.

Come back later. I can't see you now.

Doctor, Doctor, I think I'm losing my mind.

Don't worry, you won't miss it.

Doctor, Doctor, I think I'm turning
into a woman.

Well, you are 16 now Amanda.

Doctor, Doctor, I think I'm
suffering from déjà vu.

Haven't I seen you before?

Doctor, Doctor, I've got a terrible cold.
What should I do?

*Go home, take a hot bath then stand
outside in the cold with no clothes on.*

But if I do that, I'll get pneumonia.

*That's the idea. I can treat pneumonia.
I can't treat a cold.*

Doctor, Doctor, I've lost my memory.

When did this happen?

When did what happen?

Doctor, Doctor, if I give up wine, women and song, will I live longer?

No, but it will seem longer.

Doctor, Doctor, I've got jelly in my ear.

You're just a trifle deaf.

Doctor, Doctor, I think I'm a computer.

How long have you felt like this?

Ever since I was switched on!

Doctor, Doctor, my baby's swallowed some explosives.

Well, don't annoy him. We don't want him to go off.

Doctor, Doctor, my hands
won't stop shaking.

Do you drink a lot?

No, most of it spills.

Doctor, Doctor, my son swallowed
my razor-blade.

Well, just use your electric razor.

Doctor, Doctor, my wife's contractions
are only five minutes apart.

Is this her first child?

No, this is her husband.

Doctor, Doctor, should I file my nails?

No, throw them away like everyone else does.

Doctor, Doctor, since the operation
on my leg, I lean one way.

I think you're all right.

Doctor, Doctor, sometimes I feel like a goat.

How long has this been going on?

Ever since I was a kid.

Doctor, Doctor, I can't get to sleep.

*Sit on the edge of the bed and
you'll soon drop off.*

Doctor, Doctor, sometimes I feel like an onion
and sometimes I feel like a cucumber.

You've got yourself in a bit of a pickle.

Doctor, Doctor, sometimes
I think I'm a biscuit.

You're crackers.

Doctor, Doctor, sometimes I think
there are two of me.

Good, you can pay both bills on the way out.

Doctor, Doctor, tell me straight. Is it bad?

Just don't start watching any new TV serials.

Doctor, Doctor, what's wrong with me?

*Well, you've got a carrot up your nose,
a bean in one ear and a French fry in the
other. I'd say you're not eating properly.*

Doctor, Doctor, will I be able to play
the violin when my hand heals?

Of course.

Great. Because I couldn't play it before.

Doctor, Doctor, you've taken out my tonsils,
my appendix, my gall bladder and one of my
kidneys but I still feel sick.

That's enough out of you.

Doctor, Doctor, I keep seeing spots.

Have you seen an optometrist?

No, just spots.

Doctor, Doctor, I've a split personality.

Well, you'd better both sit down, then.

Doctor, Doctor, my sister keeps
thinking she's invisible.

Which sister?

Waiter, what kind of soup is this?

Bean soup.

I don't care what it's been. What is it now?

Waiter, there's a fly in my soup!

*Don't worry sir, the spider
in your salad will get it!*

Waiter, I'm in a hurry. Will my pizza be long?

No, it will be round.

Waiter, this soup tastes funny.

Why aren't you laughing then?

Waiter, this egg is bad.

Well don't blame me, I only laid the table.

Waiter, there's a bug in my soup.

Be quiet, sir or everyone will want one.

Waiter, how long will my sausages be?

Oh, about eight centimetres.

Waiter, you've got your thumb on my steak!

Well I didn't want to drop it again.

Waiter, there's a fly in my soup.

Yes sir, the hot water killed it.

Waiter, how did this fly get in my soup?

I guess it flew.

Waiter, I can't eat this meal.
Fetch me the manager.

It's no use. He won't eat it either.

Waiter, do you have frogs' legs?

Yes sir.

Then hop to the kitchen and fetch me a steak.

Waiter, I'd like burnt steak and soggy
chips with a grimy, bitter salad.

I'm afraid the chef won't cook that for you, sir.

Why not? He did yesterday.

Waiter, I'll have the burger please.

With pleasure.

No, with fries.

Waiter, I'll have the lamb chops.
And make them lean.

Certainly sir. To the right or the left?

Waiter, what is this fly doing in my soup?

Freestyle I believe.

Waiter, I'll have the soup and the fish please.

*I would recommend you eat the fish first.
It's been sitting around for a few days
and is starting to pong.*

Waiter, is there any soup on the menu?

No madam, I've wiped it all off.

Waiter, is this beef or lamb?

Can't you taste the difference?

No.

Then it doesn't matter.

Waiter, remove this fly now.

But he hasn't finished yet.

Waiter, there's a cockroach in my soup.

Sorry sir, we're all out of flies.

Waiter, there's a dead fly
swimming in my soup.

There can't be, sir. Dead flies can't swim.

Waiter, there's a flea in my soup.

Tell him to hop it.

Waiter, do you serve crabs
in this restaurant?

Yes sir, we serve anyone.

Waiter, there's a fly in my soup.

*I find that hard to believe, sir. The chef
used them all in the casserole.*

Waiter, there's a fly in my soup.

*No sir, that's a cockroach.
The fly's on your roll.*

Waiter, there's a fly in my soup.

That's because the chef used to be a tailor.

Waiter, there's a fly in my soup.

Would you prefer him in your main course?

Waiter, there's a fly on my steak.

That's because it's attracted to rotting meat.

Waiter, there's a spider in my soup.

It must have eaten the fly.

Waiter, this apple pie is squashed.

*Well, you told me to step on it
because you were in a hurry.*

Waiter, this crab has only got one claw.
It must have been in a fight.

Then bring me the winner.

Waiter, this coffee tastes like mud.

I can't understand why. It was ground
just a minute ago.

Waiter, we'll have two coffees please.
And I want a clean cup.

Yes, sir. Here are your two coffees. Now
which one of you wanted the clean cup?

Waiter, what do you call this dish?

Chicken surprise.

But I can't see any chicken?

That's the surprise.

Animal Jokes

Why are four-legged animals bad dancers?

Because they have two left feet.

Are you a vegetarian because
you love animals?

No, because I don't like plants.

What has an elephant's trunk,
a tiger's stripes, a giraffe's neck
and a baboon's bottom?

A zoo.

What does an echidna have for lunch?

Prickled onions.

Why should you never fight an echidna?

Because it will always win on points.

Why do mother kangaroos hate rainy days?

Because their kids have to play inside.

Why don't kangaroos ride bicycles?

Because they don't have thumbs to ring the little bell.

When do kangaroos celebrate their birthdays?

During leap year.

What is big and grey and out of bounds?

A tired kangaroo.

Why was the kangaroo mad at her children?

Because they were jumping on the bed.

Why did the koala fall out of the tree?

Because it was dead.

Why did the bat miss the train?

Because it spent too long hanging around.

Why do bears have fur coats?

*Because they can't get plastic
raincoats in their size!*

A grizzly bear walks into a bar
and says to the bartender, 'I'll have
a gin..........................and tonic.'

Bartender: 'What's with the big pause?'

Bear: 'I don't know. My father had them too.'

Why was the little bear spoilt?

Because he was panda'd to.

What's big white and furry and found
in outback Australia?

A very lost polar bear.

Which song do beavers sing?

'Gnawing me, gnawing you.'

What did the beaver say to the tree?

It's been nice gnawing you.

Where do bees go when they're sick?

To the waspital!

What kinds of bees fight?

Rumble Bees!

What are a bee's favourite soap operas?

*The Bold & The Bee-utiful
and Days of our Hives!*

Why was the bee's hair sticky?

Because he used a honey-comb!

What did one bee say to her
nosy neighbour bee?

'Mind your own bees' nest!'

What happened to the male
bee that fell in love?

He got stuck on his honey.

How do bees travel?

They take the buzz!

'**A** bee just stung me on the arm.'

'Which one?'

'I don't know. They all look alike to me.'

What did the teacher say
to the naughty bee?

'Bee-hive yourself.'

What do bees do with their honey?

They cell it.

What do you call a bee that buzzes quietly?

A *mumble bee.*

What is a bee's favourite meal?

A *humburger.*

What's the healthiest insect?

A *Vitamin Bee.*

What do bees wear to work?

Buzzness suits.

Where did Noah keep the bees?

In the ark hives.

What do bees use to communicate
with each other?

Their cell phone.

What do you call a woodpecker
with no beak?

A headbanger.

Which bird can never be trusted?

A lyre-bird.

Which bird can lift the heaviest weights?

A crane.

Which bird succeeds?

A budgie without teeth.

What's the definition of illegal?

A sick bird.

Did you hear about the performer who specialised in bird impressions?

He ate worms.

Which bird tastes just like butter?

A stork.

Which type of bird steals from banks?

A robin.

What do you call a bird that
lives underground?

A mynah bird.

What is a crowbar?

A place were crows go to get a drink!

Which bird is always out of breath?

A puffin.

Which language do birds speak?

Pigeon English.

What do you give a sick bird?

Tweetment.

Why does a hummingbird hum?

It doesn't know the words!

Why do birds fly south?

It's too far to walk!

What are feathers good for?

Birds.

Why is the sky so high?

So birds won't bump their heads.

Why don't baby birds smile?

*Would you smile if your mother
fed you worms all day?*

What's the difference between
a bird and a fly?

A bird can fly but a fly can't bird.

What's black and white and very noisy?

A magpie with a drum kit.

What's bright orange and
sounds like a parrot?

A carrot!

Why did the parrot wear a raincoat?

Because it wanted to be polly unsaturated.

What did the canary say when
she laid a square egg?

'Ouch!'

What's a pelican's favourite dish?

Anything that fits the bill.

What did the goose say when he got cold?

'I have people-bumps!'

What did the parrot say when it fell
in love with the frog?

'Polly wants a croaker!'

What do you get when you run a sparrow
over with a lawn mower?

Shredded tweet.

What is a polygon?

A dead parrot.

Why did the owl 'owl?

Because the woodpecker would peck 'er.

What do owls sing when it's raining?

'Too wet to woo.'

How do we know that owls are
smarter than chickens?

Have you ever heard of Kentucky-fried owl?

What does an educated owl say?

'Whom.'

What happened when the owl lost his voice?

He didn't give a hoot.

What's got six legs and can
fly long distances?

Three swallows.

What do vultures always have for dinner?

Leftovers.

What flies through the jungle singing operetta?

The parrots of Penzance.

What do baby swans dance to?

Cygnet-ure tunes.

What did the little bird say to the big bird?

'Peck on someone your own size.'

What is a parrot's favourite game?

Hide and Speak.

What do you call a Scottish parrot?

A Macaw.

How do hens dance?

Chick to chick.

What did the 100 kilo parrot say?

'Polly want a cracker, NOW!'

What do you call a well-behaved goose?

A propaganda.

When is the best time to buy a canary?

When it is going cheap.

What do parrots eat?

Polyfilla.

Why does a stork stand on one leg?

*Because it would fall over if it
lifted the other one.*

Why do buffaloes always travel in herds?

*Because they're afraid of getting
mugged by elephants.*

What did the mother buffalo say to her son
when he left for school?

'Bison.'

What's the difference between
a buffalo and a bison?

You can't wash your hands in a buffalo.

What did the caterpillar say to the butterfly?

You'll never get me up in one of those things.

Why wasn't the butterfly invited
to the dance?

Because it was a moth ball.

What does a caterpillar do on
New Year's Day?

Turns over a new leaf.

What do you call an unmarried female moth?

Myth.

What's the biggest moth in the world?

A mam-moth.

What flies around your light at night
and can bite off your head?

A tiger moth.

What do you call a camel with three humps?

Humphrey.

What do you call a camel with no humps?

A horse.

If horses wear shoes what do camels wear?

Desert boots.

Why don't cats shave?

Because they prefer Whiskas.

Why did the cat put the letter
'M' into the freezer?

Because it turns 'ice' into 'mice'.

What type of cats go bowling?

Alley cats.

Now you see it, now you don't, now you see it, now you don't. What is it?

A black cat on a zebra crossing.

ONE OF THOSE DANGEROUS
BLACK SPACES BETWEEN
THE WHITE ONES

Where do cats go for a school excursion?

The mewseum.

What looks like half a cat?

The other half.

What kind of cat loves swimming?

An octopussy.

What has four legs and flies?

A dead cat.

What do you call a cat who loses a fight?

Claude.

What happened to the cat that
swallowed a ball of wool?

She had mittens.

What do you call a cat that
lives in a hospital?

A first aid kit.

What do you call a Chinese cat that
spies through windows?

A Peking tom.

What do cats eat as a special treat?

Mice creams.

Ten cats were on a boat, one jumped off,
how many were left?

None, they were all copycats!

What did the cat say when
it lost all its money?

'I'm paw.'

What did the cat have for breakfast?

Mice bubbles.

What kind of cat shouldn't
you play cards with?

A cheetah!

'Did you put the cat out?'

'I didn't know it was on fire!'

What do you call a messy cat?

Kitty litter.

What goes '99 bonk'?

A centipede with a wooden leg.

What lies down 100 feet in the air?

A centipede.

What has 75 pairs of sneakers,
a ball and two hoops?

A centipede basketball team.

Why was the father centipede so upset?

All of the kids needed new shoes!

Why did the insects drop the centipede
from their football team?

He took too long to put on his boots!

Which side of the chicken has
the most feathers?

The outside.

Why did the chicken cross the road?

To see the man laying bricks.

Why did the goose cross the road?

To prove it wasn't chicken.

Why did the chicken cross the road, roll in
the mud and cross the road again?

Because he was a dirty double-crosser.

Why was the chicken sick?

Because it had people pox.

What is white, lives in the Himalayas
and lays eggs?

The Abominable Snow Chicken.

What do you call a crazy chicken?

A cuckoo cluck.

What do you call a chicken that
lays lightbulbs?

A battery hen.

Did you hear about the naughty chicken?

It was eggspelled from school.

What do you call the ghost of a chicken?

A poultrygeist.

Where do chickens go to die?

To oven.

Why did the chicken join the band?

Because it had drumsticks.

Why did the rooster refuse to fight?

Because he was chicken.

Why don't turkeys get invited
to dinner parties?

Because they use fowl language.

Why do chickens watch TV?

For hentertainment.

Who is the most feared animal of all?

Attila the hen.

What did Mr. and Mrs. Chicken
call their baby?

Egg.

Which hen lays the longest?

A dead one.

Why did the man cross a
chicken with an octopus?

*So everyone in his family could
have a leg each.*

What do you get when you sit under a cow?

A pat on the head.

What do you get from nervous cows?

Milk shakes.

What happened when the cow jumped over the barbed wire fence?

It was an udder catastrophe!

Why did the cow jump over the moon?

Because the farmer had cold hands.

What did the astronauts say when
they found bones on the moon?

The cow didn't make it!

What has four legs and goes 'Boo'?

A cow with a cold.

Why do cows wear bells?

Because their horns don't work!

What goes 'oom, oom'?

A cow walking backwards.

What do cows eat for breakfast?

Mooslie.

Cow 1: 'Are you concerned about catching mad cow disease?'

Cow 2: 'Not at all. I'm a sheep.'

How do cows count?

They use a cowculator.

What did the bull say to the cow?

'I'll love you for heifer and heifer.'

What do cows listen to?

Moosic.

What do you call a cow that eats grass?

A lawn mooer.

What do you call a cow that lives
at the North Pole?

An eskimoo.

What do you call cattle that always sit down?

Ground beef.

What do frozen cows do?

They give ice cream.

What game do cows play at parties?

Moosical chairs.

What is a cow's favourite film?

'The Sound of Moosic.'

What is a cow's favourite singer?

Moodonna.

Where did the cow go for its holiday?

Moo Zealand.

Where do cows go for entertainment?

The Moovies.

Which TV show do cows never miss?

The moos.

What would you do if a bull charged you?

Pay him cash.

What steps would you take
if a bull chased you?

Big ones.

What do you call a sleeping bull?

A bulldozer!

What is a crocodile's favourite game?

Snap.

What time is it when you see a crocodile?

Time to run.

Why was the crocodile called Kodak?

Because it was always snapping.

Who was the first deer astronaut?

Buck Rogers.

What do you call a deer with only one eye?

No idea.

What do you call a deer with
no legs and only one eye?

Still no idea.

What animal drops from the clouds?

A raindeer.

What did the dog say when he
was attacked by a tiger?

Nothing, dogs can't talk.

Why is a dog's nose in the middle of its face?

Because it's the scenter.

What do dogs and trees have in common?

Bark!

What do you say to a dog before he eats?

'Bone appetit!'

Why are dogs like hamburgers?

They're both sold by the pound.

What do you give a dog with a fever?

Mustard, it's the best thing for a hot dog!

What do you call a group
of boring, spotted dogs?

101 Dull-matians!

What kind of dog tells time?

A watch dog!

Where do you put a noisy dog?

In a barking lot!

What's the difference between a
well dressed man and a tired dog?

The man wears a suit, the dog just pants.

Why does a dog wag its tail?

Because no one else will do it for him.

What did the dog say when
he sat on the sandpaper?

'Rough, rough!'

What is more fantastic than a talking dog?

A spelling bee!

'Does your dog bite?'

'No.'

'Oww. I thought you said
your dog doesn't bite.'

'That's not my dog.'

Customer: 'Have you got any
dogs going cheap?'

*Pet Shop Owner: 'No, I'm afraid
they all go woof.'*

Did you hear the one about the dog running ten kilometres to retrieve a stick?

It was too far-fetched.

'I play Scrabble with my pet dog every night.'

'He must be clever.'

'I don't know about that. I usually beat him.'

'I've lost my dog.'

'Put an ad in the paper.'

'Don't be silly. He can't read.'

How do you know when
it's raining cats and dogs?

You step into a poodle.

How do you stop a dog doing
his business in the hall?

Put him outside.

When is a brown dog not a brown dog?

When it is a greyhound.

Where would you find a dog with no legs?

Exactly where you left it.

What happened to the dog that
swallowed the watch?

He got ticks.

Why did the dog cross the street?

To slobber on the other side.

What's the difference between a barking dog and an umbrella?

You can shut the umbrella up.

What do ducks watch on TV?

Duckumentaries.

What kind of doctor treats ducks?

A quack.

Did you hear about the duck decorator?

He papered over the quacks.

Customer: 'How much for the duck?'

Pet shop owner: '$20.'

Customer: 'I only have $15.
Can you send me the bill?'

*Pet shop owner: 'No, you'll have
to take the whole duck.'*

What's another name for a clever duck?

A wise quacker!

What happens when ducks fly upside-down?

They quack up.

Why did the duck go ring-ring?

He got a phone bill.

Which birds steal the soap from the bath?

Robber ducks.

What's the difference between a gym instructor and a duck?

One goes quick on its legs and the other goes quack on its legs!

How do ducks play tennis?

With a quacket.

What is a duck's favourite TV show?

The feather forecast.

What do you call a crate of ducks?

A box of quackers.

What did the duck say to the comedian after the show?

'You really quacked me up!'

What do you call a duck with fangs?

Count Quackula.

What do you get when you cross
an elephant with a fish?

Swimming trunks!

What do you get when an elephant
sits on your friend?

A flat mate.

What do you call an elephant
in a telephone box?

Stuck.

What do you call an elephant
that never washes?

A smellyphant.

How do you get six elephants
in a fire engine?

Two in the front, two in the back and two on
top going 'Eeeeawww, eeeeawww'.

What do you give a sick elephant?

A very big paper bag.

Why do elephants live in the jungle?

Because they can't fit inside houses.

Why are elephants wrinkled all over?

Because they can't fit on an ironing board.

What's the difference between
an elephant and a flea?

*An elephant can have fleas but a
flea can't have elephants.*

What time is it when an elephant
sits on your fence?

Time to get a new fence.

What did Thomas Edison Elephant invent?

The electric peanut.

'**H**ave you ever found an elephant
in your custard?'

'No.'

'It must work then!'

Why did the elephant paint the
bottom of his feet yellow?

So he could hide upside down in custard

What did Tarzan say when he saw the
elephants coming over the hill?

Here come the elephants over the hill.

What do a grape and an elephant
have in common?

They're both purple, except for the elephant!

How do you fit an elephant into a matchbox?

Take out the matches!

How do you fit a tiger into a matchbox?

Take out the elephant!

'Did you know that elephants never forget?'

'What do they have to remember?'

Why is a snail stronger than an elephant?

A snail carries its house, and an elephant
only carries his trunk!

Why is an elephant large,
grey and wrinkled?

Because if it was small, white and
smooth it would be an aspirin!

How can you tell an elephant from a banana?

*Try to lift it up. If you can't, it's either an
elephant or a very heavy banana.*

What game do elephants play
in a Volkswagen?

Squash!

How does an elephant get down from a tree?

He sits on a leaf and waits for autumn.

Why do elephants' tusks stick out?

Because their parents can't afford braces!

Where can you buy ancient elephants?

At a mammoth sale.

How do you stop an elephant from smelling?

Tie a knot in his trunk.

What's bright blue and very heavy?

An elephant holding its breath.

What's the same size and shape as an elephant but weighs nothing?

An elephant's shadow.

How do you get an elephant up an acorn tree?

Sit him on an acorn and wait twenty years.

Why are elephants grey?

So you can tell them apart from canaries.

How do you get down from an elephant?

*You don't get down from an elephant,
you get down from a duck.*

What do elephants have that
no other animal does?

Baby elephants.

What's the difference between an African
elephant and an Indian elephant?

About 6000 kilometres.

What's the difference between a mouse
and an elephant?

About a ton.

Why do elephants never get rich?

Because they work for peanuts.

What time is it when an elephant
climbs into your bed?

Time to get a new bed.

What do elephants take when
they can't sleep?

Trunkquilisers.

Which animals were the last to leave the ark?

*The elephants – they were
packing their trunks.*

'**M**y dad is so short-sighted that he can't get
to sleep unless he counts elephants!'

How do you get an elephant into a car?

Open the door.

How does the elephant get out of the car?

The same way it got in.

How do you know when there is
an elephant in the oven?

You can't close the door.

How do you know when an elephant
has been using your phone?

You've been charged for trunk calls.

How do you know peanuts are fattening?

Have you ever seen a skinny elephant?

How do you know when there is
an elephant in the fridge?

There are footprints in the butter.

Why can't an elephant ride a tricycle?

*Because it doesn't have thumbs
to ring the bell!*

What did the mouse say to the elephant?

Squeak.

Did you hear about the elephant
that drank a bottle of rum?

He got trunk.

Why do elephants have wrinkled knees?

From playing marbles.

What do you call an elephant that
flies straight up?

An elecopter.

What do you call an elephant that flies?

A jumbo jet.

What do you call the red stuff between an elephant's toes?

A slow hunter.

What do you give an elephant with diarrhoea?

Plenty of room.

Why do elephants have wrinkles
on their skin?

Because they've stayed in the bath too long.

What is big, grey and wears glass slippers?

Cinderelephant.

What is grey with sixteen wheels?

An elephant on roller-skates!

Where do elephants go on holidays?

Tuscany.

Why do elephants have Big Ears?

Because Noddy wouldn't pay the ransom.

Why do elephants have trunks?

Because they can't fit everything
into a handbag.

Why do elephants wear sneakers?

So they can sneak up on mice.

Why was the elephant standing
on the marshmallow?

He didn't want to fall in the hot chocolate.

Where do baby elephants come from?

Very big storks.

Why did the zookeeper refuse to work in the elephant enclosure?

Because the work kept piling up.

What is big, green and has a trunk?

An unripe elephant.

How do goldfish go into business?

They start on a small scale.

What is an octopus's favourite song?

'I want to hold your hand, hand, hand, hand, I want to hold your hand, hand, hand, hand.'

What does an octopus wear when it's cold?

A coat of arms.

What do you call a neurotic octopus?

A crazy, mixed-up squid.

What's the difference between
a piano and a fish?

You can tune a piano, but you can't tuna fish!

What's slimy, tastes of raspberry,
is wobbly and lives in the sea?

A red jellyfish.

How does a jellyfish race start?

Get set.

What did the fish say when he
swam into the wall?

Dam.

What do you call a fish with no eyes?

Fsh.

Where do sharks shop?

The fish market.

What do you call a Russian fish?

A Tsardine.

What kind of fish can you find in a birdcage?

A perch!

Why did the fish cross the sea?

To get to the other tide.

Why did the fish jump out of the water?

Because the seaweed.

What is a little fish's favourite TV show?

Plaice School.

What type of fish is always sleeping?

A kipper.

What do you call a baby whale that
never stops crying?

A little blubber.

Where would you weigh a whale?

At a whale-weigh station?

What does a crab use to call someone?

A shellular phone!

What do you do with a blue whale?

Try to cheer him up!

What do you call a baby whale?

A little squirt.

What shouldn't you do when
you meet a shark?

Go to pieces.

What do you call the autobiography
of a shark?

A fishy story.

Why did the shark take so long
to eat a victim's arm?

*Because the victim's watch made
it time consuming.*

Why was the crab arrested?

Because it kept pinching things.

What lives at the bottom of
the sea with a six gun?

Billy the Squid.

What's an eel's favourite song?

'Slip Sliding Away.'

What kind of sharks never eat women?

Man eating sharks.

What do frogs order in restaurants?

French Flies!

What do you call a frog with no legs?

Unhoppy.

What did the croaking frog
say to her friend?

'I think I've got a person in my throat.'

How did the frog die?

It Kermit-ted suicide.

What do you say to a hitchhiking frog?

'Hop in.'

What is a frog's favourite drink?

Croaka-cola.

What is green and hard?

A frog with a machine gun.

What is Kermit the Frog's middle name?

The.

What's white on the outside,
green on the inside and hops?

A frog sandwich.

Where do musical frogs perform?

At the Sydney Hopera House.

Why can't frogs get life insurance?

Because they are always croaking.

What is green and loud?

A froghorn.

Why did the frog throw away the book?

Because he'd reddit (read it).

Why do frogs like beer?

Because it is made from hops.

What is a tadpole after it is five days old?

Six days old.

What happened to two frogs that caught
the same bug, at the same time?

They got tongue-tied.

Where do tadpoles change into frogs?

The croakroom.

What are teenage giraffes told when
they go on their first date?

No necking.

What did the giraffe say when a car
load of tourists drove past?

'It's terrible the way they're caged up.'

What's the tallest yellow flower in the world?

A giraffodil.

Why do giraffes have long necks?

Because their feet stink.

What do you call a young goat who
visits a psychiatrist?

A mixed-up kid.

Why can't you have a conversation
with a goat?

Because it always butts in.

What is small, brown and squirts jam?

A hamster eating a doughnut.

What do you call a hippo that believes in peace, love and understanding?

A hippie-potamus.

What can go as fast as a race horse?

The jockey!

What has four legs and sees just as well from both ends?

A horse with his eyes closed.

What do you call a pony with a sore throat?

A little horse!

How do you hire a horse?

Put four bricks under his feet.

Where do horses stay in a hotel?

In the bridle suite.

How do you make a slow racehorse fast?

Put it on a diet.

What disease do you have if you're
allergic to horses?

Bronco-itis.

What do you give to a horse
with a sore throat?

Cough stirrup.

Where do sick ponies go?

To the horsepital.

Why do horses only wear shoes?

Because they would look silly with socks on.

Which TV show do horses like best?

Neigh-bours.

What do you call a fly with no wings?

A walk.

What did one firefly say to the
other before he left?

'Bye! I'm glowing now!'

Why did the fly fly?

Because the spider spied her.

What has four wheels and flies?

A wheelie bin.

Why were flies playing football in a saucer?

They were playing for the cup.

Why did the flies run across the top
of the cling wrap box?

Because it read 'Tear along the dotted line.'

What do you call a fly when it retires?

A flew.

What's the difference between
a mosquito and a fly?

Try zipping up a mosquito!

What did the mosquito say when
he saw a camel's hump?

'Gee, did I do that?'

What do you call a mosquito that
prefers walking to flying?

An itch-hiker.

What has six legs, bites,
buzzes and talks in code?

A morse-quito.

Why did the firefly get bad grades in school?

He wasn't very bright!

How do fireflies start a race?

Ready, steady, glow!

How do you start a flea race?

One, Two, Flea, Go!

What do you call a mad flea?

A looney-tic!

What did one flea say to the other?

'*Shall we walk or take the dog?*'

What is the biggest ant in the world?

An eleph-ant.

What's even bigger than that?

A gi-ant!

How many ants are needed to
fill an apartment?

Ten-ants.

Where do ants eat?

A restaur-ant.

What is smaller than an ant's mouth?

An ant's dinner.

Why don't anteaters get sick?

Because they're full of ant-ibodies.

Name six things smaller than
an ant's mouth?

Six of its teeth!

What do termites eat for dessert?

Toothpicks.

What is a termite's favourite breakfast?

Oak-meal.

What did the termite say when she saw that her friends had completely eaten a chair?

Wooden you know it!

Why did the termite quit its job?

Because it was boring.

Which insects can tell the time?

Clockroaches.

Which movie character do insects like best?

Bug Lightyear.

Why is the letter 'T' important
to a stick insect?

Because without it, it would be a sick insect.

Why did the lion feel sick after
he'd eaten the priest?

Because it's hard to keep a good man down.

What did the lioness say to the
cub chasing the hunter?

'Stop playing with your food.'

Why did the lion spit out the clown?

Because he tasted funny.

Funny Insults

You are so dumb you planted birdseed because you wanted to raise canaries.

You are so dumb you gave cough syrup to your pony because someone told you it was a little horse.

You are so dumb you fed money to your cow because you wanted to get rich milk.

You are so dumb you wore a wet shirt
all day because the label said
'wash and wear'.

You are so dumb you ate yeast and shoe
polish for breakfast because you wanted
to rise and shine in the morning.

You are so dumb you run around and
around your bed so you can catch up
with your sleep.

You are so dumb you got fired from
your job as an elevator operator because
you couldn't remember the route.

You are so dumb you think a cartoon is something you sing in the car.

You are so dumb you tripped over a cordless phone.

You are so dumb you burnt your ear because you were ironing when the phone rang.

You are so dumb you burnt your other
ear when the caller rang back.

You are so dumb, when you tried to
make a birthday cake the candles melted
in the oven.

You are so dumb you take your bicycle
to bed because you don't want to walk
in your sleep.

Janet: 'What's the difference between a
cake and a school bus?'
Jill: 'I don't know.'
Janet: 'I'm glad I didn't send you
to pick up my birthday cake!'

You are so dumb you think a buttress is a female goat!

You are so dumb you threw away your guitar because it had a hole in it.

You are so dumb you told your teacher you couldn't write an essay on goldfish because you didn't have any waterproof ink.

You are so dumb you got fired from the banana factory for throwing out all the bent ones.

My gym teacher is so dumb he runs around the exam rooms hoping to jog students' memories.

You are so dumb you think Hamlet is an omelette with bacon.

'**O**ur teacher talks to herself in class, does yours?'

'*Yes, but she doesn't realize it. She thinks we're listening!*'

Student: 'I don't think I deserve a zero on this test.'

Teacher: 'No, neither do I but it was the lowest I could give you!'

You are so dumb you think software is a floppy hat.

Ben's teacher thinks Ben is a wonder child.

She wonders whether he'll ever learn anything.

Teacher: 'That's the stupidest boy in the whole school.'

Mother: 'That's my son.'

Teacher: 'Oh! I'm so sorry.'

Mother: 'You're sorry?'

'How old would you say I am, Francis?' the teacher asked.

'Forty,' said the boy promptly.

'What makes you think I'm forty?' asked the puzzled teacher.

'My big brother is twenty,' he replied, 'and you're twice as silly as he is!'

You are so dumb you saw a moose's head hanging on a wall and went into the next room to find the rest of it!

You are so dumb you kept banging your head against the wall because it felt so good when you stopped.

You are so dumb you went round and round in a revolving door looking for the doorknob.

You are so dumb you think a polygon is a dead parrot.

You are so dumb you invented a parachute that opens on left-handed screwdriver.

You are so dumb you invented a one-way escalator.

You are so dumb you could be brainwashed with an eyedropper.

You are so dumb you invented a chocolate teapot.

You are so dumb you invented
waterproof teabags.

You are so dumb you invented a
parachute that opens on impact.

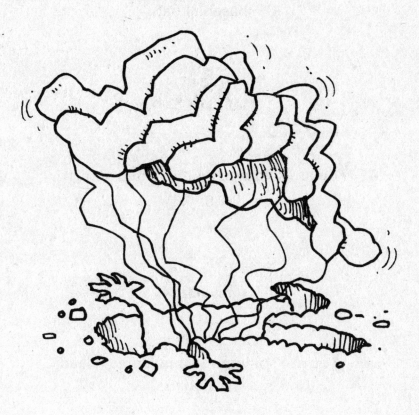

You are so dumb you invented a fly screen on a submarine.

You are so dumb you invented a glass baseball bat.

You are so dumb you invented a mirror for ghosts.

You are so dumb you invented a lead balloon.

You are so dumb you invented a solar-powered torch.

You are so dumb you invented an ashtray for a motorbike.

You are so dumb you invented black windows.

You are so dumb you invented rubber nails.

You are so dumb you invented an
ejector seat on a helicopter.

You are so dumb you invented non-stick
glue.

You are so dumb you invented sugar
cube fishing bait.

You are so dumb you invented a bikini
for Eskimos.

You are so dumb you invented
underwear for kilt wearers.

You are so dumb you ate a worm when
you were asked to do a bird impression.

You are so dumb you turned away from Disneyland after seeing a sign that read 'Disneyland Left'.

You are so dumb you got fired from the M&M factory for throwing away all the W's.

You are so dumb you climbed over a glass wall to see what was on the other side.

You are so dumb you think that a kilo of feathers weighs less than a kilo of lead.

You are so dumb you got your money back after having your mind read.

You are so dumb you called your pet zebra 'Spot'.

Boy: 'They say ignorance is bliss.'

Girl: 'Then you should be the happiest boy in the world!'

Everyone calls you 'Fog' because you are dense and wet.

You are so dumb you take a pencil to bed to draw the curtains.

Boy: 'I'll tell you everything I know.'

Girl: 'In that case you'll be speechless!'

You are so dumb you write letters to your grandpa slowly because he can't read very fast.

You are so dumb you jump up and down before taking medicine because the label reads 'Shake well before using'.

Dick and Jane were arguing over the breakfast table.

'Oh, you're so stupid!' shouted Dick.

'Dick!' said their father. 'That's quite enough! Now say you're sorry.'

'Okay,' said Dick. 'Jane, I'm sorry you're stupid.'

You are so dumb your computer has
whiteout all over the screen.

You are so dumb, you saw a sign
outside a police station that read
'Man Wanted for Robbery', and
went in and applied for the job!

You are so dumb you think a fjord is a Scandinavian motor car.

You are so dumb, when you went hitchhiking you got up early so there wouldn't be much traffic around.

You are so dumb, when I asked you what the weather was like, you replied, 'It's too foggy to tell.'

You are so dumb, when the lifesaver told you not to jump in the pool because there was no water, you replied, 'It's alright, I can't swim.'

You are so dumb, when you bought a train ticket and the ticket seller asked, 'Where to?' you replied, 'Back here of course!'

You are so dumb, when you held up the music store you told them to give you the lute.

You are so dumb, when you went shoplifting you stole a free sample.

You are so dumb you fell out of a tree after you were told to rake up the leaves.

You are so dumb, when you tried to do some glass blowing you inhaled and got a pane in the tummy.

You are so dumb, when you flew a helicopter you turned the propeller off because you couldn't stand the draft.

You are so dumb, when your Greek mythology teacher asked you to name something that was half-man and half-beast, you replied, 'Buffalo Bill'.

You are so dumb, when I told you that your shoes had to be soled, you sold them.

You are so dumb, when you went
shoplifting you hurt your back trying to
lift the corner store.

You are so dumb, when you dress up as
a pirate you put a patch over both eyes.

You are so dumb, if you ever have a
brain transplant, the brain will be sure
to reject you.

Your dad is so dumb, when he locked his keys in the car he called a mechanic to get the family out.

You are so dumb you slept under your car because you wanted to wake up oily in the morning.

You are so dumb you spent two hours in a department store looking for a cap with a peak at the back.

You are so dumb, when you went skiing you skied up the slope and caught the chair lift down.

You are so dumb at Halloween you carve a face on an apple and go bobbing for pumpkins.

You are so dumb you have a stop sign at the top of your ladder.

You are so dumb, when you went water-skiing you spent your whole holiday looking for a sloping lake.

Your uncle, Farmer Peter is so dumb he packed up and moved to the city when he heard that the country was at war.

You are so dumb you got seventeen of your friends to accompany you to the movies because you heard it was not for under-18s.

You are so dumb you left your job as a telephonist because you kept hearing voices.

You are so dumb you took a gun with you when you went white-water rafting, so you could shoot the rapids.

You are so dumb you fell in the sink
while tap dancing.

You are so dumb you threw away your
doughnut because it had a hole in the
middle.

Your dad is so dumb he walked into the
electricity company with a $20 note in
each ear because he received a bill
saying he was $40 in arrears.

Your dad is so dumb he only gets a half-hour lunch break because if he took any longer he would have to be re-trained.

Our goalkeeper is so dumb he won't catch the ball because he thinks that's what the net is for.

How many toes does an idiot have?

Take off your socks and count them.

You are so dumb you forgot your twin brother's birthday.

Don't let your mind wander — it's too little to be let out alone.

You are so dumb you put stamps on the faxes that you send.

With you here, your village must be missing its idiot.

You would be out of your
depth in a puddle.

You are not as stupid as you look.
That would be impossible.

I'd leave you with one thought if you
had somewhere to put it.

You are so dumb it takes you an hour to
cook one-minute noodles.

You are so dumb you think the English Channel is a British TV station.

You are so dumb you took your mobile phone back to the shop because it came without a cord.

If someone offered you a penny for your thoughts, they'd expect some change.

You are so dumb you leapt from a
window to try out your new jump suit.

You should go to a dentist and have
some wisdom teeth put in.

You have an open mind.
Ideas just slip straight out.

You are so dumb you stared at the orange juice container because it said 'Concentrate'.

You are so dumb it takes you three hours to watch 'Sixty Minutes'.

Your dad is so dumb he took a ruler to bed to see how long he slept.

Your dad is so dumb he sold his car for gas money.

You are so dumb you can't
pass a blood test.

Your brother is so dumb, when he
swam across the English Channel he
got tired half way and swam back.

You are so dumb you put a chicken in a
hot bath so it would lay hard-boiled
eggs.

Your mum is so dumb she put lipstick
on her forehead because she wanted to
make up her mind.

You are so dumb you asked for a price check at the $2 shop.

Your mum is so dumb, when you asked her to buy you a colour TV she asked, 'What colour?'

Your dad is so dumb he locked himself
in a motorbike.

Your granddad is so dumb he got
locked in a supermarket overnight
and died of starvation.

Your grandma is so dumb, when the
sign said 'Don't Walk' she froze and got
hit by a bus.

You are so dumb you order a
cheeseburger without cheese.

Your mum is so dumb, when she
fills in forms that say 'Sign Here',
she writes 'Taurus'.

You are so dumb you threw the butter
out of window because you wanted to
see a butterfly.

You are so dumb you tried
to drown a fish.

You are a few clowns short of a circus.

You are a few fries short
of a Happy Meal.

You are an experiment
in artificial stupidity.

You are a few beers short of a six-pack.

You are a few peas short of a casserole.

You are one Fruit Loop
shy of a full bowl.

You are as smart as bait.

You are so dumb you wear two
sets of pants when you play golf
in case you get a hole in one.

Your elevator doesn't go all
the way to the top floor.

You forgot to pay your brain bill.

Your sewing machine is out of thread.

Your antenna isn't picking
up all the channels.

'I've changed my mind.'

'Great, does the new one work any better?'

How do you make a stupid person
laugh on a Thursday?

Tell him a joke on Monday.

'How dare you tell everyone I'm stupid.'

'Sorry, I didn't realise it was a secret.'

How can you kill a dumb
person with a coin?

Throw it under an oncoming truck.

You are so dumb you put your
pet cat next to the computer to
keep an eye on the mouse.

The cat that made off with the mouse... and the computer

'Do you find me entertaining?'

'You're too dim to entertain a thought.'

I hear you were the last one born in
your family. I can understand that.
You're enough to discourage anyone.

You are so dumb you put a coin
in a parking meter and waited
for a gumball to come out.

You are so dumb, when you missed the
44 bus you took the 22 twice instead.

You are so dumb you ordered
your sushi well done.

You are so dumb you invented a solar
powered flashlight.

You are so dumb you got
hit by a parked car.

You are so dumb you thought Sherlock
Holmes was a housing project.

You are so dumb you bought a horse because you wanted to play water polo.

You are so dumb you called the 24-hour supermarket to see when they closed.

You are so dumb, when you heard 90% of all accidents occur around the home you moved.

I like you a lot. But then, I've never had good taste.

You are so dumb you bought a
video camera to record cable
TV shows at home.

Calling you stupid would be an
insult to stupid people.

Go ahead, tell us everything you know.
It'll only take 10 seconds.

You are a monument to the human
race. And you know what pigeons
do to monuments.

He has a mind like a steel trap –
always closed!

He is living proof that man can live
without a brain!

He is the kind of a man that you would
use as a blueprint to build an idiot.

He's not stupid; he's possessed by a
retarded ghost.

You are so dumb you went to night
school to learn to read in the dark.

I bet your brain feels as good as new,
seeing that you've never used it.

I don't know what makes you so stupid,
but it really works!

I don't think you are a fool. But then
what's my opinion against thousands
of others?

I heard you went to have your
head examined but the doctors
found nothing there.

I know you are nobody's fool but maybe
someone will adopt you.

You are so dumb you tiptoe past the medicine cabinet so that you don't wake the sleeping pills.

I would ask you how old you are but I know you can't count that high.

I'd like to leave you with one thought . . . but I'm not sure you have anywhere to put it!

If I ever need a brain transplant,
I'd choose yours because I'd want
a brain that had never been used.

You're so unpopular even your
answering machine hangs up on you.

If what you don't know can't hurt you
you'll live forever.

If you stand close enough to him
you can hear the ocean.

If your brain was chocolate it
wouldn't fill an M&M.

Keep talking, someday you'll say
something intelligent.

You are so dumb you refused to buy a
ticket for the door prize because you
already have a door.

So a thought crossed your mind? Must have been a long and lonely journey.

There is no vaccine against stupidity.

Just because you have a sharp tongue does not mean you have a keen mind.

Are you always this stupid or are you making a special effort today?

Brains aren't everything. In fact in your case they're nothing.

You have a photographic mind. It's a pity it has never been developed.

You look lost in your thoughts — unfamiliar territory for you.

You don't know the meaning of the word 'fear', but then again you don't know the meaning of most words.

You are so dumb you tried to fit a cake into a typewriter so you could write 'Happy Birthday'.

You are the kind of friend a person can depend on. You're always around when you need me.

You do the work of three men:
Larry, Curly & Moe.

You are so dumb you threw a rock at
the ground, and missed.

You are so dumb if you had a brain
you'd take it out and play with it.

You're a miracle of nature. You have an IQ of 2 and you're still able to speak.

If you were any dumber you'd have to be watered twice a week.

You're so dumb you can't even spell the word 'dumb'.

You are so dumb you couldn't pour water out of a boot if the instructions were written on the bottom of the heel.

You are so dumb you put your socks on inside out because there was a hole on the outside.

I'll try being nicer if you try being smarter.

The closest you'll ever come to a
brain storm is a light drizzle.

You are so dumb you couldn't find
your butt if both your hands were
tied behind your back.

It's perfectly all right to have an
unexpressed thought. In fact, in
your case I recommend it.

I would never enter into a battle of wits

with an unarmed person.

You are so dumb you think martial arts

are paintings by the sheriff.

You obviously fell out of the Stupid Tree

and hit every branch on the way down.

You know I do understand you. I seem
to have a way with dumb animals.

You are so dumb you think people who
live in Paris are called parasites.

People say you're a perfect idiot: I tell
them you may not be perfect but you are
doing a great job being an idiot.

You are so dumb you think birds that are kept in captivity are called jail birds.

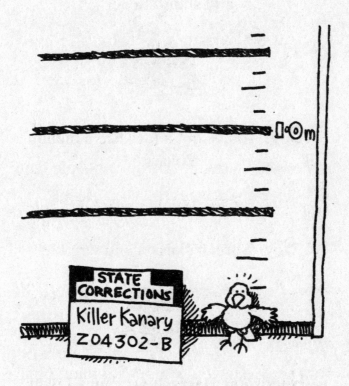

You are so dumb you push when playing tug of war.

You are so dumb, when you call your
dog you put two fingers in your mouth
and shout 'Rover'.

Boy: 'You've got a face like a million
dollars.'

Girl: 'Have I really?'

Boy: 'Sure, it's green and wrinkly!'

Handsome Harry: 'Every time I walk
past a girl, she sighs.'

Wisecracking William: 'With relief!'

Everyone has the right to be ugly, but you abused the privilege.

Bill: 'My sister has lovely long hair, all down her back.'

Will: 'Pity it's not on her head!'

Woman: 'When I'm old and ugly, will you still love me?'

Man: 'I do, don't I?'

What's small, annoying and really ugly?

I don't know but it comes when I call my sister's name.

'**M**y sister went on a crash diet.'

'Is that why she looks a wreck?'

Every time I take my girlfriend out for a meal, she eats her head off.

She looks better that way.

You are so ugly, when you went on a package tour near where headhunters live you were the only survivor.

Turn the other cheek. On second thoughts, don't. The view is just as ugly on that side.

You are so ugly, when you enter a room the mice jump on chairs.

You are dark and handsome. When it's
dark you are handsome.

Last time I saw someone as ugly
as you I had to pay admission.

You are so ugly the only dates you get
are on a calendar.

You are so ugly you have to trick
or treat over the phone.

Doctor, Doctor, I have a hoarse throat.

The resemblance doesn't end there.

Your mum is so ugly she went
to a beauty salon and it took
three hours . . . for an estimate.

Your sister is so ugly the garbageman
won't even pick her up.

'Haven't I seen you on TV?'

'Well yes, I do appear off and on.
How do you like me?'

'Off.'

Don't look out of the window. People
will think that it's Halloween.

After cruel taunts about
having a head like a
pumpkin... Peter opted
for a quiet night in
on Halloween.

'**D**o you think that I'll lose my looks
when I get older?'

'With luck, yes.'

'**M**y husband always carries my photo in his pocket. It once saved his life when a mugger tried to stab him.'

'Your face would stop anything.'

Doctor, Doctor, I'm so ugly what can I do about it?

Hire yourself out for Halloween parties.

Every time you open your mouth your foot falls out.

'I've just come back from the beauty salon.'

'What a pity it was closed.'

I'm not saying my wife isn't good looking but when she goes to the doctor he tells her to open her mouth and go 'Moooo'.

'What would it take to make me look good?'

'A lot of distance between you and me.'

'**B**oys fall in love with me at first sight.'

'I bet they change their minds
when they look again.'

'**S**hall I put the TV on?'

'Well it would certainly improve
the view in here.'

You are so ugly, when you joined an
ugly contest they said, 'Sorry, no
professionals allowed.'

You are so ugly, when you were
born your mother said, 'What a
treasure!' and you father said,
'Yes, let's go bury it.'

You are so ugly they push your face into
dough to make cookies.

You are so ugly even Rice Bubbles
won't talk to you!

'**D**addy, Daddy, there's a monster at the
door with a really ugly face.'

'Tell him you've already got one!'

You are so ugly people go as you to
Halloween parties.

You are so ugly the government moved
Halloween to your birthday.

You are so ugly they didn't give you
a costume when you auditioned
for Star Wars.

You are so ugly, when you try to take a
bath the water jumps out!

You are so ugly, when you walk
into a bank they turn off the
surveillance cameras.

You are so ugly you could
turn Medusa to stone!

You are so ugly you won the prize for
best costume at the Halloween Party
even though you were just picking up
your sister.

You are so ugly you made an onion cry.

You are so ugly your mum had to tie
a steak around your neck to get the
dog to play with you.

You are so ugly your mum had to get
drunk to breast feed you.

You mum is so ugly I heard that your
dad first met her at the pound.

You mum is so ugly on Halloween the kids trick or treat her by phone!

Your mum is so ugly they pay her to put her clothes on in strip joints.

You mum is so ugly your father takes her to work with him so that he doesn't have to kiss her goodbye.

If I were as ugly as you I'd wear a mask.

You're so ugly, when a wasp stings
you it has to shut its eyes!

Don't you need a licence to be that ugly?

You are so ugly, when you were a
baby your mum had to feed you
with a slingshot.

You are so ugly, when you stand on the
beach the tide won't come in.

You are so ugly, when you were
born the doctor turned you over
and said, 'Look. Twins.'

Your face is so ugly it would make a
train take a dirt road.

Either you're very ugly or your
neck has stepped in something.

Your sister has everything a
man desires — bulging muscles
and moustache.

Your sister is so ugly she was asked to

remove her mask at a masked ball —

and she wasn't wearing one.

Your feet are so smelly your shoes

refuse to come out of the closet.

You might not know much but you

lead the league in nostril hair.

Teacher: 'Billy, stop making ugly faces at the other students!'

Billy: *'Why?'*

Teacher: 'Well, when I was your age, I was told that if I kept making ugly faces, my face would stay that way.'

Billy: *'Well, I can see you didn't listen.'*

'I've kept my youthful complexion.'

'So I see, all spotty.'

'**W**hy are you bathing in
such dirty water?'

'It wasn't dirty when I got in.'

'**Y**ou smell funny.'

*'That's my soap. I don't suppose
you've smelt it before.'*

'**I**s that a new perfume I smell?'

'It is, and you do.'

What's the difference between
you and a wild camel? One is a
big, smelly, bad tempered beast
and the other is an animal.

I've heard you're the big noise around
here. I think you should cut back on the
baked beans.

You don't need to use an insult, you
could just use your breath.

First Boy: 'Do you keep yourself clean?'

Second Boy: 'Oh, yes, I take a bath every
month, whether I need one or not!'

Your breath is so bad that people look
forward to your farts.

Your mum is so fat a picture
of her fell off the wall!

Your mum is so fat all the restaurants in
town have signs that say: 'Maximum
Occupancy: 200 Patrons OR Your Mum'.

Your mum is so fat at a restaurant
when they give her the menu she
replies, 'Yes please.'

Your mum is so fat Bill Gates couldn't afford to pay for her liposuction.

Your mum is so fat Dr Martens needed three cows just to make her a pair of shoes.

Your mum is so fat every time she puts an apple in her mouth people try to roast her.

Your mum is so fat her belly jiggle is the first ever perpetual motion machine.

Your mum is so fat her belt is the size of the equator.

Your mum is so fat her cereal bowl came with a lifeguard.

Your mum is so fat her clothes have stretch marks.

Your mum is so fat her high school year
book picture was an aerial picture.

Your mum is so fat her picture
takes two frames.

Your mum is so fat I had to take
a train and two buses just to get
on her good side.

Your mum is so fat instead of wide leg jeans, she wears wide load.

Your mum is so fat she can lie down and stand up and her height doesn't change.

Your mum is so fat she had her baby pictures taken by satellite.

Your mum is so fat she had her ears
pierced by harpoon.

Your mum is so fat she has
her own area code.

Your mum is so fat she has more chins
than the Chinese phone book.

Your mum is so fat she has to
buy two airline tickets.

Your mum is so fat she has two
stomachs . . . one for meats and one
for vegetables.

Your mum is so fat she makes Big Bird
look like a rubber duck.

Your mum is so fat she makes
Free Willy look like a tic tac.

Your mum is so fat she makes sumo
wrestlers look anorexic.

Your mum is so fat she needs a hula
hoop to keep up her socks.

Your mum is so fat she needs a
watch on both arms because she
covers two time zones.

Your mum is so fat she sets off car
alarms when she runs.

Your mum is so fat she was born with a
silver shovel in her mouth.

Your mum is so fat she
shows up on radar.

Your mum is so fat she went
on a seafood diet . . . whenever
she saw food she ate it.

Your mum is so fat she went to the
movies and sat next to everyone.

Your mum is so fat she's got smaller fat
women orbiting around her.

Your mum is so fat she's on
both sides of your family.

Your mum is so fat she's like the
Bermuda Triangle; when kids run
around her they get lost.

Your mum is so fat the horse on her
Polo shirt is real.

Your mum is so fat the last time she saw
90210 was on the scale.

Your mum is so fat they had to grease
the bathtub to get her out.

Your mum is so fat they tie a
rope around her shoulders and
drag her through a tunnel when
they want to clean it.

Your mum is so fat, when her
beeper went off they thought
she was backing up.

Your mum is so fat, when I tried to
drive around her I ran out of gas.

Your mum is so fat, when she bends
over we lose an hour of daylight.

Your mum is so fat, when she bungee jumps she brings down the bridge too.

Your mum is so fat, when she goes to a restaurant she doesn't get a menu she gets a quote.

Your mum is so fat, when she goes to an all you can eat buffet they have to install speed bumps.

Your mum is so fat, when she gets in an
elevator it has to go down.

Your mum is so fat, when she goes to
the circus she sees the big top and asks,
'Where can I try that on?'

Your mum is so fat, when she
leaves the beach everybody shouts,
'The coast is clear.'

Your mum is so fat, when she
runs she makes the CD player
skip . . . at the radio station.

Your mum is so fat, when she sits on the
beach Greenpeace shows up and tries to
tow her back into the ocean.

Your mum is so fat, when she steps on the scale it says, 'One at a time please.'

Your mum is so fat, when she steps on the scale it says, 'Sorry we don't do livestock.'

Your mum is so fat, when she tiptoes everyone yells, 'Stampede!'

Your mum is so fat, when she turns around they throw her a welcome back party.

Your mum is so fat, when she walked in front of the TV I missed three commercials.

Your mum is so fat, when she was diagnosed with the flesh eating disease the doctor gave her five years to live.

Your mum is so fat, when she went to
get a water bed they put a blanket
across the Pacific Ocean.

Your mum is so fat, when she
went to the beach she's the
only one who got a tan.

Your mum is so fat, when the police
showed her a picture of her feet she
couldn't identify them.

Your mum is so fat your bathtub
has stretch marks.

Your mum is so fat she climbed
Mt Everest with one step.

Your mum is so fat, when she
fell in love she broke it.

There's nothing wrong with you
that death wouldn't cure.

Go and sit down. Nobody can stand you.

'You'd make a good exchange student.'

'Do you think so?'

'Yes we might be able to exchange you
for someone nice.'

'**Y**ou remind me of a camel.'

'Why?'

'You give me the hump.'

If we were to kill everybody who
hates you, it wouldn't be murder;
it would be genocide!

I'm not being rude, you're just
insignificant.

You were so annoying on the
airline flight that the steward
told you to go and play outside.

Doctor, Doctor, everyone hates me.

*Don't be stupid, not everyone
has met you yet.*

Waiter, do you serve crabs
in this restaurant?

Yes sir, we serve anyone.

You are so lazy you got a job in a
bakery to have a good loaf.

He's good at everything he does. And as
far as I can see he usually does nothing.

You're so lazy, that if you woke up with
nothing to do, you'd go to bed with it
only half done.

'Mum, there's a man at the door
collecting for the Old Folks' Home,'
said the little boy.

'Shall I give him Grandma?'

Jane: *'Do you like me?'*

Wayne: *'As girls go, you're fine and
the sooner you go, the better!'*

A girl walked into a pet shop and said,
'I'd like a frog for my brother.'

'Sorry,' said the shopkeeper. 'We don't do
exchanges!'

First Man: 'My girlfriend
eats like a bird.'

Second Man: 'You mean she hardly eats a
thing?'

First Man: 'No, she eats slugs and
worms.'

'**D**o you think, Professor,
that my girlfriend should
take up the piano as a career?'

'*No, I think she should put down
the lid as a favour!*'

'**M**y brother's been practising
the violin for ten years.'

'*Is he any good?*'

'No, it was nine years before he found
out he wasn't supposed to blow!'

James: 'I call my girlfriend Peach.'

John: *'Because she's soft,
and beautiful as a peach?'*

James: 'No, because she's
got a heart of stone.'

When Wally Witherspoon proposed to
his girlfriend, she said, 'I love the simple
things in life, Wally, but I don't want one
of them for a husband!'

Maria: 'Whatever will Tammy do when
she leaves school? She's not smart
enough to get a job!'

Leonie: *'She could always be a
ventriloquist's dummy.'*

My girlfriend talks so much that when she goes on vacation she has to spread suntan lotion on her tongue!

Jane: 'Do you ever do any gardening?'

Wayne: 'Not often. Why?'

Jane: 'You look as if you could do with some remedial weeding.'

'Can I go swimming now, Mum?'
asked the child.

'No – there are sharks at this beach,'
said his mother.

'Dad's swimming!'

'Yes, he's got a million dollars' life insurance.'

A woman woke her husband in the
middle of the night.

'There's a burglar in the kitchen eating the
cake I made this morning!' she said.

'Who should I call?' asked her husband.
'The police or an ambulance?'

My big brother is such an idiot. The other day I saw him hitting himself over the head with a hammer. He was trying to make his head swell, so his hat wouldn't fall over his eyes!

A man walks into a bar with a skunk under his arm.

Barman: 'You can't bring that smelly thing in here.'

Skunk: 'Sorry. I'll leave him outside.'

Person 1: 'I've never been so insulted in all my life.'

Person 2: 'You haven't been trying.'

'Waiter, I'd like burnt steak and soggy chips with a grimy, bitter salad.'

'I'm afraid the chef won't cook that for you, sir.'

'He did yesterday.'

'Mummy, Mummy, Dad has been run over by a steamroller.'

'Shut up and slide him under the door.'

'Mummy, Mummy, Daddy's on fire.'

'Hurry up and get the marshmallows.'

'Mummy, Mummy, why do I keep
going round in circles?'

'Shut up or I'll nail your other
foot to the floor.'

'Mummy, Mummy, are you sure you
bake bread this way.'

'Shut up and get back in. I can't
close the oven door.'

'Mummy, Mummy, Dad's going out.'

'Shut up and throw some
more petrol on him.'

'Mummy, Mummy, Daddy's
hammering on the roof again.'

'Shut up and drive a bit faster.'

'Mummy, Mummy, why is Dad running
in zig zags?'

'Shut up and keep shooting.'

'**M**um, why do I have to go to school?
The kids all make fun of me and
all the teachers hate me.'

'Because you're the headmaster, son.'

'**M**ummy, Mummy, why are we
pushing the car off the cliff?'

'Shut up or you'll wake your father.'

What do you call a guy who hangs
around musicians?

A drummer.

'This piece of music is haunting.'

'That's because you're murdering it.'

'What shall I sing next?'

'Do you know Bridge
Over Troubled Waters?'

'Yes.'

'Then go and jump off it.'